CW01645184

CIRCLES OF ADULTS

A team approach to problem solving around challenging behaviour and emotional needs.

by Derek Wilson and Colin Newton

Published by Inclusive Solutions UK Ltd

Published by Inclusive Solutions UK Limited
January 2006
Images by Derek Wilson
Design by Chloe Bowles (www.fivebeans.co.uk)
Printed by Parker & Collinson Ltd
ISBN 0-9546351-2-4

CONTENTS

FOREWORD

Circle of Adults is an in depth problem solving process intended to support teams of adults in schools who work with young people with emotional and behavioural difficulties. Using group processes and graphic facilitation, the members are guided through a set of key questions to reach a deeper understanding of the young person's challenging behaviour, unmet needs and to develop new strategies. As a teacher, I think one of the main advantages of this method is that it leads to an increased understanding not only of the emotional needs of the children but also those of the adults who work with the most challenging young people. Prior to being a participant in Circle of Adults meetings, I felt there were few professional opportunities, in the schools I had taught at, to share anxieties that arose from teaching pupils who had emotional and behavioural difficulties with other colleagues in a safe and constructive way. The Circle of Adults process offers a clear structure and a stimulating experience to allow adults to support and extend their work with young people who have emotional and behavioural difficulties.

The first Circle of Adults meeting I participated in was focused around a child in Year 5, who I had been supporting in a school within my role as an outreach teacher for MAST, (part of the Behaviour Support Service aimed at reducing the number of 10-13 year old pupils from being permanently excluded). To protect his confidentiality I will refer to him as John.

John had been in care for most of his life and had had more than thirty different care placements in ten years. Not surprisingly, his behaviour in school was erratic, often threatening towards staff and pupils and showed a disregard for adults in authority. When I first met John he was crawling around the classroom pretending to be an animal, whilst the rest of the class was quietly reading. Although I had 9 years of teaching experience behind me, this child's behaviour had challenged me the most. The week before the Circle of Adults meeting I had been hit by John at the end of his session. This occurred as I had turned off the computer he was using at the time I had said I would, when John himself had wanted to continue. At the time I understood that the child's behaviour wasn't a personal attack but was about him wanting control and had buried my own feelings of hurt so I could be strong enough to work with John the next day.

However, at the Circle of Adults meeting I met John's key workers, social worker and family friend and recognised that other adults had experienced the same difficulties that I had. This was extremely reassuring and helped me to feel safe to express those feelings of exhaustion and emptiness that I had felt after the incident. The facilitator's careful questioning helped me to recognise that the feelings I experienced were probably John's too. The strategy part of the meeting was inspiring; I felt heard, valued and respected for my ideas and I was also able to seek advice about how to use a new strategy, guided imagery. I left the meeting feeling nurtured and excited, as well as having more space to build empathy and understanding for John. The following week I used guided imagery with John, which he responded well to. This intervention resulted in a referral for John to receive play therapy.

My experience in Circle of Adults meetings made me realise the value and importance of teachers' personal needs being met in order to meet those of the most difficult children they teach, which inspired me to make the Circle of Adults process the focus of my dissertation for the MA in Human Relations Course. This provided me with the opportunity to interview staff from an Education Support Centre that had recently participated in a Circle of Adults meeting. One of the most interesting findings was that each of the teachers interviewed found that the Circle of Adults affected a degree of change either in themselves or what they observed in other colleagues. For one Teaching Assistant the Circle of Adults meeting enabled her to become more objective in her attitude towards the child's behaviour and this then enabled her to change the way she worked with the child in the future. She commented:

> **"The meeting made you draw back, by being able to separate the behaviour you know it's not directed at you, so it makes you feel better about what you're doing, so you don't react in the same way, you don't get so angry."**

Circle of Adults meetings also seem to have the potential for long-term impact for both the child and the adults working with them. One of the teachers I interviewed described it in these terms:

> **"It affected the staff's relationship with the child, we felt like we'd invested a lot in him and we really wanted him to succeed."**

The outcome for this particular child was also positive. The Head decided not to permanently exclude him and instead reduced the child's timetable.

I am convinced that the Circle of Adults process can support and inspire those adults who are committed to helping children who are the most difficult to reach. I base this not only on my own experiences as a teacher, but also based on feedback from teachers, learning mentors, counsellors and outside agencies who have participated in other circles. Comments have included:

> **"It helped me step back and reflect, I feel more in control of the situation."**
> (Primary Learning Mentor)
>
> **"The process was useful in getting a fuller overview of the contexts the child exists in and how he might be feeling."** (School Counsellor)
>
> **"Inspirational and enriching."** (SENCO)
>
> **"I'm clear where I am now and where I need to go to help the child."** (Primary Teacher)

Perhaps the reason for these positive outcomes for both the child and the adult lie in the following account:

> **"We are only in a position to give when our own needs go some way to being acknowledged and satisfied. To give when we feel like we have something to give and not just when the client demands."** Hawkins and Shohet 1989:14

Sarah Stockley, Team Leader
Multi-Agency Support Team, Nottingham City LEA.

INTRODUCTION

What you will find in this book is a fresh approach - Circle of Adults - to figuring out how to make effective provision for children and young people with challenging behavioural and emotional needs. It is primarily a book about the effective facilitation of others' problem solving efforts and is a tool that is particularly well suited to the work of multi-disciplinary teams. The aim of the Circle of Adults process is to help the frontline person - usually the class teacher, form tutor, residential social worker, year manager etc - deepen their understanding of the young person causing concern and use this deeper understanding to generate new strategies for support.

"A truly inclusive school has structures for making space and time - it knows what to do when you don't know what to do"

John O'Brien 2002

Circle of Adults is a robust facilitation tool that has been thoroughly road tested by the authors in a range of educational settings and with a wide range of different professionals. We can confidently say that, properly facilitated, the process works.

Another way of thinking about the Circle of Adults process is that it provides a forum for group supervision. This is a source of support for front line workers that is notably absent in most of our educational settings. Few school managers in the UK have been able to put together a reliable, organised and effective means of support for their staff. This is despite the (well publicised) demands on staff trying to meet the emotional and behavioural demands of their students. Over the last 15 years there have been a number of successful attempts by LEA support service staff to address these unmet supervision needs - see Stringer et al (1992), Newton (1995), Farouk (2004) and very recently - Spohrer and Cooke (2005), Evans (2005). A common thread running through all of these initiatives is the debt they owe to the work of Gerda Hanko - this book is no exception and we examine this debt in detail below.

The Circle of Adults process generates multiple perspectives on the issue that is brought to the group and is therefore ideal for use with a multi-disciplinary team. However the entire process is carefully boundaried by the facilitators in a way that leaves no scope for taking sides or indulging in arguments and 'turf wars' over who is 'right' - the final word lies with the problem presenter and what he or she decides to take forward from the session.
The process takes up to 90 minutes to complete and is therefore a tool that you are only likely to use when things are serious; where people don't know what to do next, are feeling they have 'tried everything' and there is talk of permanent exclusion and/or segregated placements.

Circle of Adults is not the answer for people trying to live with others' challenging behaviour; it is a process, a means, an approach to finding solutions or a better way. But there are no guarantees, only the hope that a thoughtful process, carefully facilitated, may lead to deeper understandings, a strengthening of the person who has brought the issue to the circle and some new ways forward.

The Circle of Adults process aims to provide opportunities for:

Aims

Key staff and managers should understand these

- Shared problem solving in a safe exploratory climate in which the group will find its own solutions.
- Individuals to reflect on their own intervention methods and receive feedback from the group.
- An exploration of whole-school or organisational processes and their impact on individual staff attempting to meet pupil needs.
- Emotional support and shared understandings of issues at a pupil, family, school and community level.
- Feed back to school staff on issues, ideas and strategies that are agreed to be worth sharing with them.

Psychodynamic Insights

In developing the Circle of Adults approach we have drawn on a number of sources. A primary source of inspiration was the work of Gerda Hanko (Hanko 1999, 2002). Many of the guiding ideas within this book are drawn from her key text: *'Increasing Competence through Collaborative Problem Solving'* (1999). One of Gerda's gifts is her capacity to import psychodynamic insights into her facilitation. She has been able to do this in an accessible way and without recourse to the esoteric jargon that can make this field of knowledge hard to use.
In 2002 (pp380-381) Gerda Hanko summarised the essence of a psychodynamic understanding of hard to manage behaviour as follows:

'Practising teachers may better understand the psychodynamic base if they come to realise:

- That children with problem behaviour are experiencing feelings that they find difficult to bear, but that behaviour is more likely to be managed to the extent to which these feelings are understood by those who are involved with them.

- That children's difficult here and now behaviour (whether displayed overtly or masked in over-compliance or withdrawal) is a likely reaction to a present situation they perceive as 'unmanageably' difficult because it echoes similar past events in damaging relationships. (For instance a teacher's reprimand, even if justified, may fit into a past pattern of being rejected, not feeling valued, believing themselves to be inherently dislikeable; just as a teacher's well meant praise may lead to an outburst of despair in children who, believing themselves to be 'born stupid', may irrationally fear having to disappoint a teacher who appears to believe in them.

- That a child's behaviour in the classroom is further influenced by our response to it and, in its turn, further influences ours. Thus the trained professional's response may be a major influence on whether the interaction becomes a virtuous or a vicious cycle.'

The range of insights and understandings that makes up the body of psychodynamic knowledge is not easy to access or source. It lies scattered across a number of key texts and writings, many of which are hard to obtain or out of print. Psychodynamic perspectives on human emotional development are not widely taught within educational psychologists' training nor within initial or advanced teacher training.

This body of knowledge is barely referenced within the huge (and daily growing) number of books and practice manuals that address behaviour management for teachers and schools systems and the absence is especially marked in the North American literature on behavior. Indeed our knowledge of the psychodynamic perspective on young people's behaviour and emotion is decidedly piecemeal and no doubt contains many gaps and omissions.

So we apologise in advance for our selective use of psychodynamic insights and the likely loss of many nuances and subtle tones.*

Footnote:

*Contrast the above insights with those provided by the behaviourist/behaviour modification mindset that still seems to be the default setting of much of what is taught on the theme of 'behaviour management'. The 'insights' provided by the behavioural model were incisively summarised by Herb Lovett (1996) in his seminal work on understanding difficult behaviour - 'Learning to Listen'.

'The informing syllogism of behaviour modification is that reinforcers, defined as anything that increases behaviour, increase behaviour; and punishments, defined as anything that decreases behaviour, decrease behaviour. By manipulating rewards and punishments, behaviour can be changed'

Herb would have us note that this is 'an intellectual construct…so slight as almost not to exist' Learning to Listen p. xvi.

Another strong critic of the rewards and punishments mindset is Alfie Kohn and his provocatively titled book 'Punished By Rewards' (1999) is little known in the UK.

Kohn offers a clear challenge to some of our most deep seated assumptions about what makes people tick.

If you want to create a fairly instant consensus around this debate; ask any group of adults with responsibility for the care and control of children - 'What about those who do not respond even to praise?'

Both Herb Lovett and Alfie Kohn are keen to take their readers on a journey from control to collaboration and thereby increase their effectiveness in responding to challenging behaviour. The Circle of Adults process, relying as it does on collaborative staff teams, is well placed to help us on that journey.

Insights and Practices from Person Centred Planning Approaches

Another huge influence on the Circle of Adults approach has been the person centred facilitation work of Jack Pearpoint, Marsha Forest and John O'Brien (see O'Brien and O'Brien 2002 for an overview of this field of work). Our experiences in using person centred planning tools such as MAPS and PATH (as well as the smaller scale group problem-solving tool - 'Solution Circles') led us to recognise the importance of co-facilitation when working with the complexity of process generated by groups meeting to problem solve around behaviour. Our person centred planning work also led to the introduction of graphic facilitation to the Circle of Adults process. You will find the full beginners guide to graphic facilitation further on in this book.

> **"In an inclusive school, teachers encourage students to face real problems in the common life of their classroom with the clear expectation that they will make a significant contribution to figuring out what to do and how to do it."**
>
> John O'Brien- Inclusion as a Force for School Renewal

A Developing Tool

If you read the first published account of the Circle of Adults process (Newton 1995), it will be clear that the tool has been added to and reshaped in the intervening 10 years. Openness to new influences wherever these seem to make the tools you use more robust is a key part of professional development. We expect this reshaping to continue and that we will regularly incorporate participants' improvement suggestions whenever these appear to contain a new or creative insight.

Circle of Adults addresses problems further upstream than conventional approaches to problem solving. It targets change at the source of our thoughts and feelings around a particular young person or difficult issue.

Footnote:

It would be a mistake to assume that the Circle of Adults process is solely intended for use around children and young people with a label of emotional and behavioural difficulties. To do this would be to perpetuate the damaging myth that disabled children do not have an emotional life. The best exploration of this myth and its effects continues to be: 'Mental Handicap and the Human Condition' by Valerie Sinason, Free Association Books 1992. The fact is we have facilitated many successful Circles of Adults sessions where the young people being thought about have had many different types of labels assigned to them.

A QUICK GUIDE

Circle of Adults is a group problem solving tool that gives a deeper understanding of emotional and behavioural needs in a school or organisational context and for planning actions to meet those needs. To use this tool you will need:

- A Group of people - all with a stake in the issue who have the time and the belief in the possibility that there is more we can understand about a child or young person to enable us to do better.
- Two people to facilitate the process.
- Time to meet without interruptions.

The process

- Uses both process and graphic facilitation to give the session clear structures (with negotiated and agreed ground rules) and timings. Up to 1 hour 15 minutes is the minimum generally required to complete all the steps in the process. It is not an invitation to have an open ended 'discussion' about a child or young person. A member of the group is chosen who will listen to the emerging story from the child's perspective. Later in the process this person will be asked to feedback their thoughts and feelings as the 'Child's Voice'.
- Asks guiding questions designed to capture the emotional complexity and interactive nature of challenging behaviour. It seeks to understand 'behaviour' as an aspect of adult-child relationship and not as something solely about or within the child.
- Fully explores the interactive aspects of the challenging situation and in particular the quality of the problem presenter's relationship with the young person.

- Is explicit about the emotional drivers - adults' and child's - underlying the issue and seeks to get a better understanding of these.
- Considers the system and organisational factors that are perceived by the group to be either helping or hindering the present situation.
- Looks to build on the existing strengths of the problem presenter as perceived by the group.
- Listens to the feedback from the 'Child's Voice'.
- Does ALL OF THE ABOVE before it:
    - Uses the collective capacity of the group to generate strategies and fresh ways forward on the issue. These strategies are explicitly linked to the hypotheses and understandings developed earlier in the process and not simply a range of off-the-shelf and well worn solutions with no obvious linkage to the hypotheses generated. In a school setting, strategies that use the curriculum in therapeutic ways are actively encouraged.
    - Concludes the problem solving process by designing a series of specific 'first steps' that the problem presenter will take in the next few days and appoints a coach from within the group to check in with the problem presenter on how things went.
    - Concludes the group's time together by asking for a 'round of words' that reflects each member's experience of the process.

THE ROLE OF THE FACILITATOR

A Circle of Adults session is co-facilitated and this is a key aspect of its effectiveness. The two facilitators work together to ensure that the problem solving group remains on track and completes its work in the time available. The facilitators' 'expertise' lies in their capacity to effectively stage manage the process through each of its 10 steps. It is seldom, if ever, that they will contribute to the content of the session. The 10 steps of the process can usefully be imagined as 10 'containers' which the facilitators place before the group and invite them to fill. Each step is boundaried and once a step is completed the group should be discouraged from going back and adding to or amending what has been said. This allows the facilitators to maintain the forward momentum of the process and increases the chance of finishing on time with all steps completed.

Dealing with the cynic

Most staff teams have their resident cynic or two. Their role is to remind others why it can't work, that it has already been tried and made no difference - they don't see the point. Sometimes they will be present, often on sufferance, at a Circle of Adults session and can present various kinds of challenges to the facilitators. We have found various ways to minimise their potential for sabotage. The first is to get your ground rules tight, agreed and then to enforce them. The cynic is usually pretty obvious from the start - if only through their body language - and that can be the facilitators' cue to ensure the declared ground rules are robust enough to keep the process on track and diffuse negativity. A powerful ground rule is 'The Law of Two Feet' which says that 'if during the course of the session, any person finds him or herself in a situation where they are neither learning nor contributing, they must use their two feet and go to some more productive place' (Owen 1997) This simply invites the cynic to go on his or her way (taking their negative energy with them) and do something they deem more useful. The Law of Two Feet is a very freeing strategy to have in place from the facilitators' point of view; in our experience it is seldom, if ever, acted upon but its introduction at the start sets the tone for what is to follow.

Of course there will always be those who sit through a Circle of Adults session and never really seem engaged with the process. Often monosyllabic in their contributions, they are clearly reserving their judgement on the usefulness of any outcomes. We like to tell ourselves that these participants, if they have listened even a little, will find it near impossible to see the young person in the same way as they did before the session and that there will likely be small changes in their approach to the child and these may well be positive. Herb Lovett's advice is helpful in reminding us why certain members of the team may find it hard to engage with the process:

> **"Many of us avoid things because:**
> **We fail to see the point**
> **We feel the demand is unfair**
> **It makes us feel inadequate"**
>
> Herb Lovett - Learning to Listen 1996

The Circle of Adults process is designed to address each of the above reasons why people may not be in a position to respond in different ways to a young person whose needs are not currently being met.

About Facilitation

This book is mainly about group facilitation skills and should provide the reader with a firm grounding in both 'process' and 'graphic' facilitation. The teaching of group facilitation is still novel in the UK for those aiming to work in local authority or other services that seek to support schools and other settings in achieving meaningful and creative solutions to the issues confronting them. Nor are facilitation skills given any explicit reference in the recent and major DfES (2005) initiative - The National Programme for Specialist Leaders of Behaviour and Attendance. With over 30 separate training units making up this programme, not one is explicitly about group facilitation.

Equally, the extensive literature on group facilitation (see Kaner 1996, Holman and Devane 1999) for excellent summaries of this field) is not widely known or referenced within the UK literature on strategies for behaviour management/meeting special educational needs.

> **"I see group facilitation as a whole constellation of ingredients: a deep belief in the wisdom and creativity of people; a search for synergy and overlapping goals; the ability to listen openly and actively; a working knowledge of group dynamics; a deep belief in the inherent power of groups and teams; a respect for individuals and their points of view; patience and a high tolerance for ambiguity to let a decision evolve and gel; strong interpersonal and collaborative problem solving skills and a flexible versus a lock step approach to resolving issues and making decisions."**
>
> Michael Doyle - Forword to Facilitator's Guide to Participatory Decision-Making 1996

This is all the more surprising given the increasing emphasis in UK education policy on the creation of integrated childrens services in which multi-disciplinary teams are expected to work together ever more closely to achieve coherent outcomes for children and families. It is not hard to see how the group facilitator's 'constellation of ingredients' referred to in Micheal Doyle's quote on page 13 might be relevant in this arena.

The two guiding lights of group facilitation and therefore of the Circle of Adults process are:

- People need to participate in and own the solutions to the problems confronting them and if they don't, then implementation will be half-hearted at best and most likely will fail.

- A key factor in any successful school is its capacity to elicit, harness and focus the creativity and goodwill that is always resident in its staff members. Sometimes this is known as the organisation's 'intellectual capital'. Once it is energised and released the school can become a powerful force for positive change.

"..the primary role of the expert is one in which they facilitate, with others, the construction of a contextually relevant truth, one that may not generalise to other contexts."

J Moore 2005

Circle of Adults is not the answer for people trying to live with others' challenging behaviour. It is a process, a means, an approach to finding solutions or a better way. But there are no guarantees, only the hope that a thoughtful process, carefully facilitated, may lead to deeper understandings, a strengthening of the person who has brought the issue to the circle and, for them, some new ways forward.

> **"'Human being' is more a verb than a noun. Each of us is unfinished, a work in progress. Perhaps it would be most accurate to add the word 'yet' to all our assessments of ourselves and each other. Jon has not learned compassion ...yet. I have not developed the courage ...yet. It changes everything. If life is a process all judgements are provisional. We can't judge something until it is finished. No one has won or lost until the race is over."**
>
> Rachel Naomi Remen, 'Kitchen Table Wisdom'

GRAPHICS

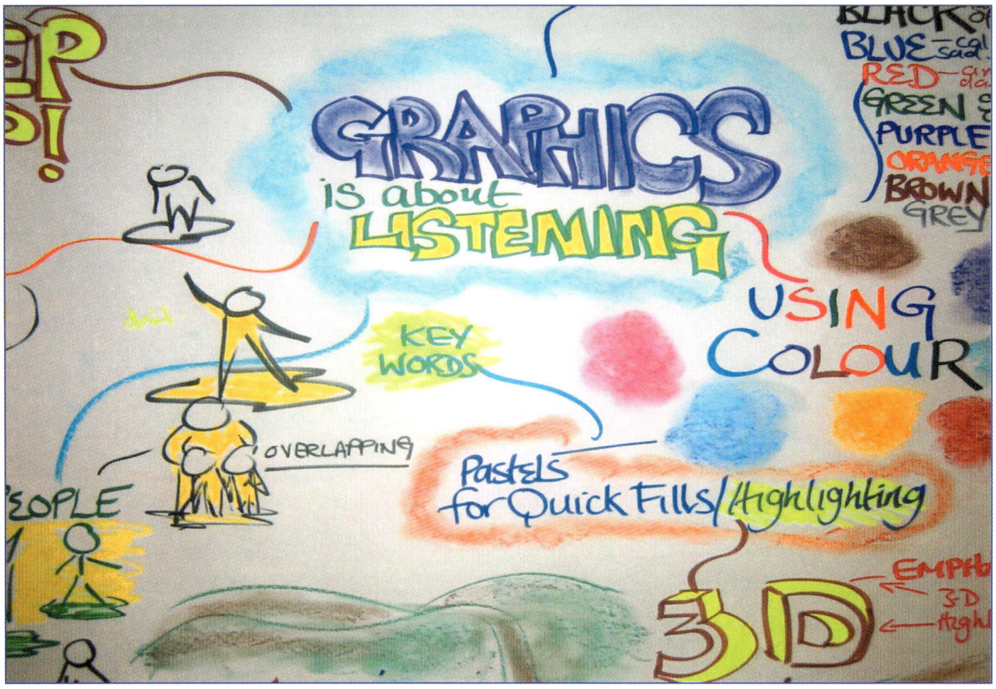

Why Graphics?

If you have to ask this question you probably need to do more graphic facilitation. The short answer is because it works.
We don't think the 'reasons why' have yet been fully explored but here are some likely candidates:

- Visual learning and attention is activated - the graphic endures and develops throughout the course of the Circle of Adults session (whereas spoken words may fade and get forgotten) Participants can literally 'see what each other means'.
- A graphic embodies complexity and connection much more efficiently than speech alone.
- Participation by ALL is enhanced - each can see that they have been heard/listened to and their contributions accepted and recorded.
- **COLOUR** is used to reflect meaning and emotion.
- The PAST, PRESENT, and the FUTURE can be seen in the same frame. A faithful graphic record of a Circle of Adults session will contain information on what has happened with the problem in the past, how things are now and some future steps designed to bring about change.
- Graphic facilitation allows time and space for those who process meetings differently. If you need 15 minutes to organize your response to a part of the graphic, this time is usually available.
- With a graphic you can go back and correct, modify, add to - mistakes are usually OK - in fact they are often part of the evolving meaning.
- A graphic encourages the group to build on each other's ideas rather than refute/challenge and is therefore more likely to develop consensus.

General Coaching Prompts

Paper and Pens: A typical graphic size is around 4'x5' and it is worth having the outlines/headings of the first 2/3 Steps marked on the paper before you begin the session proper. Remember that Steps 1, 2 and 3 will occupy half the available time for the circle of adults session (1hour and fifteen minutes is a minimum for the full process including setting the tone and closure) and therefore half the paper needs to be set out for these three steps.

Starting: It often makes most sense for the graphic facilitator to give the group an overview of the 10 steps in the Circle of Adults process.

It is important to remind the group not to wait for you to write everything down - graphic facilitation is not a verbatim recording of what was said. Your aim is to capture the essence of what took place at each step. Let the group know that you will check back regularly to ask if anything has been missed/inadequately represented.

Resist the urge to précis/paraphrase or interpret when you are recording. The key words/images should be the group's own. However you can help individuals in the group (particularly the problem presenter) clarify an important word or image by asking for the detail - e.g. What would it look like? What colours are you seeing?

Summarising: At the completion of each step of the process the graphic recorder can briefly summarise what has been recorded, both to check for any misunderstandings or identify underdeveloped areas. Whether or not you decide to do this is a judgement call. There probably won't be time to do a summary at the end of each step, but if you feel that the group's contributions within a particular step have been hard to record or somewhat woolly, then pushing for more clarity by way of a summary can be helpful. The graphic facilitator is also expected to provide a synthesis as Step 6 of the Circle of Adults process and this will be discussed below.

Keep Up! This is the first priority in the graphic facilitator's mind. He or she must keep pace on the graphic with what is being talked about in the group. Once you start to fall behind and/or miss parts of the discussion then you are in trouble and the resulting graphic record will not do what you want it to.

Use All the Paper - As the graphic facilitator you need to be mindful that by the end of the process you should have filled *all* the paper. Leaving an empty piece in the bottom left hand corner lessens the impact of the graphic and suggests 'unfinished business'.

Colour

Effective use of colour to amplify and to add emotional tone to what a graphic is saying within certain words or sections is one key to successful facilitation. Colours have associations. Some are personal, many are shared within particular cultures and some, but by no means all (e.g. Yellow is associated with 'Caution' in North America) go across cultures. As a graphic facilitator you need to bring these shared associations to a conscious level and be able to think on your feet what colour might do best for any particular part of the Circle of Adults graphic. But a note of caution here - the rule book on this is vague and intuitive at best, often the most helpful idea is to ask the problem presenter/group what colour they are seeing this part of the graphic - especially during Steps 2 and 3 - 'Present Problem' and 'Exploring Relationships' - as these are the steps most likely to have clear emotional content. Some associations to the main colours you are likely to use are listed below - there are many others.........

Blue Cool temperature/calming, blue sky, big picture, trust, authority and reliability. Blue is one of the key colours of any graphic because of its association with trust and reliability - Try and use more than one shade of Blue.

Purple Denotes 'importance', something highly valued, royalty, wine, the good life, religion/mysticism.

Red Alarm, danger, heat/hot line, stop sign, emergency, marked errors (red pen)/'in the red', fire. A good colour for underlining, adding ticks to items where there is agreement, recording areas of tension and 'feelings' words at key points in the graphic. Caution: Use relatively sparingly, - too much Red is hard to look at and can act as a barrier to people's engagement with the graphic.

Green "GO!" recycling, nature, money, growth, new life, creativity.

Yellow Sunny, ideas and invention, optimism. CAUTION! Do not use Yellow as the main colour for lettering or images - it cannot be easily seen at a distance - Use instead as a fill colour for the inside of objects or block lettering, or as a pastel 'wash' for parts of the graphic. Yellow can also be used to make 'notes to yourself' somewhere on the margins of the graphic. These notes in Yellow can be read close up by you but are illegible at a distance to the group. Such notes are a useful way of storing up the key themes you want to feed back in Step 6 - 'Synthesis'.

Brown Earth, groundedness, foundations and underpinning ideas. Powerful in combination with green in suggesting the natural world.

Orange Fruit, sun, liveliness! Sunsets, fireworks and excitement. Try to use a fairly dark orange for use in a graphic. Like yellow, Orange can be hard to see at a distance.

Black Best used as a 'neutral' colour, for facts or data. Problematic if used to denote negativity/'bad' scenarios - may provoke a challenge you don't need. Consider use of 'grey' instead - using thick pencil lead as an option.

Pictures and Symbols

It is not essential to use just images when doing the graphic - a strong visual picture can be created using variations in colour (including pastel shading), lettering style and size. However use of imagery will heighten the impact of the graphic and the fact is that a single image can capture the essence of an idea/vision in an immediate way and this is helpful in 'buying time' for the graphic facilitator as well as focusing the group on a shared idea. Reassure yourself that a drawing need only be 30% accurate to be recognizable, you do not have to suddenly become an artist to do graphic facilitation.

Use arrows within the graphic to create forward flow and connection.

It is worth developing a stock of key images that you have practised and can draw reasonably quickly - Milly Sonneman's book "Beyond Words - a guide to drawing out ideas" Ten Speed Press 1997 is an excellent source of tips on developing your set of basic images as is Jack Pearpoint's 'Hints for Graphic Facilitators'. Inclusion Press 2002.

> **"I learned that simple drawings worked the best, and that a drawing only needed 30 percent of reality to be recognisable."**
>
> Milly Sonneman - 'Beyond Words' (1997)

Lettering

In lettering, as with so many things in life, **size matters**. First and foremost your lettering on the graphic needs to be readable by all the group. Absolute size will depend on how big your group is - before the session starts, take a minute to stand at the back of the room and look at your poster and give yourself an idea of the general letter size that will be needed. Caution! - take care not to use lettering that is **too big** - you don't have the space and you risk having participants feeling pushed out by the graphic.

Lettering is fundamental to a successful graphic. Think of lettering as pictures that just happen to be words and experiment with the full range of lettering options as well as doing things with your lettering of key words so that they express meaning or emotion. Again Milly Sonneman's book is a good source of guidance on lettering options.

Finally...

It's all about practice. No one is born able to do graphic facilitation. It's not about being able to draw well, it's about being able to listen and capture what happens in the Circle of Adults session in a way that facilitates the group's efforts and provides an adequate record of their planning. Like in the learning of any new skill, practice and your improvement is inevitable!

Graphics Supplies

Paper Roll: A typical Circle of Adults graphic measures about 5 feet long by 4 feet deep. It is worth investing in a good quality Art-Craft roll of paper like that supplied in the UK by Hope Education. £35.00 will buy you a big enough roll for at least 25 individual graphics.

Masking Tape: For hanging the graphic to the wall. Buy the widest tape you can get - it gives you the best chance that your paper will actually stay up on the wall for the full session!

Marker Pens (chisel tipped)

Highlighter Pens

Soft Pastel Crayons or Chalks

Digital Camera: Because each graphic is unique and very large, it is not possible for each participant in the session to have a hard copy of what took place. One way round this is to take a digital image of the graphic at the end of the session and circulate this either by email or as a printed copy to all who took part.

"The graphic is not just an add on. It is an essential component...The images and colour switch on parts of our brains that we don't use regularly, and thus help us to think differently and more creatively."

Marsha Forest and Jack Pearpoint reflecting on the power of graphics in 'PATH - A Workbook for Planning Positive Possible Futures' (2001)

Examples

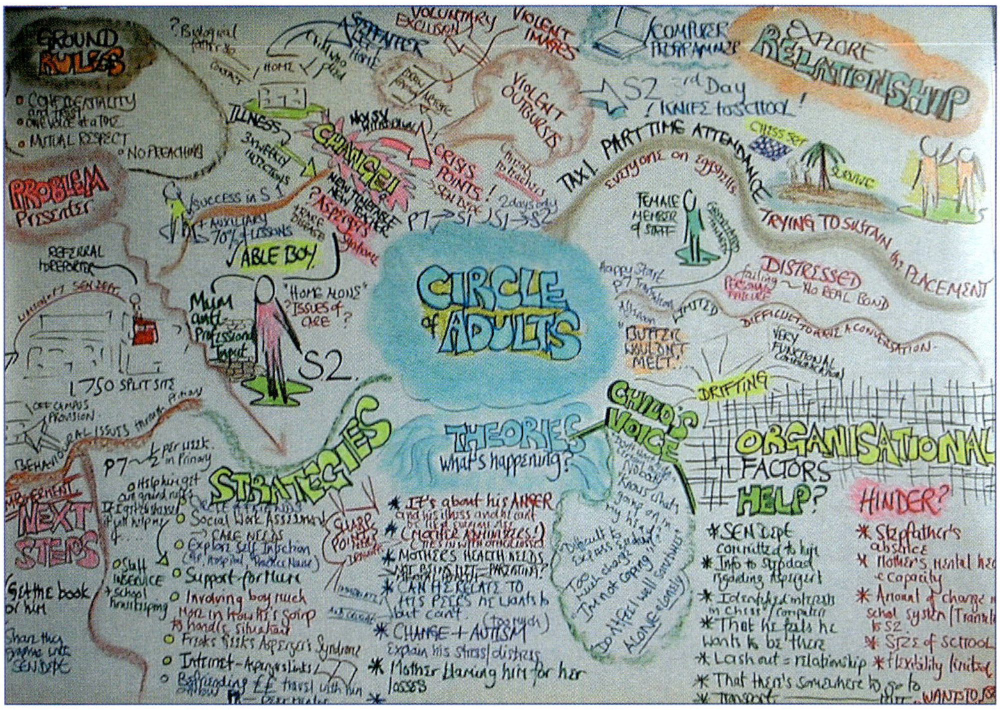
GROUND RULES
CONFIDENTIALITY
MUTUAL RESPECT
NO PREACHING
PROBLEM Presenter
VOLUNTARY EXCLUSION
VIOLENT IMAGES
COMPUTER PROGRAMMER
EXPLORE RELATIONSHIP
VIOLENT OUTBURSTS
CRISIS POINTS
KNIFE to school
PART TIME ATTENDANCE
TRYING TO SUSTAIN the PLACEMENT
ABLE BOY
FEMALE MEMBER of STAFF
DISTRESSED
S2
CIRCLE of ADULTS
1750 SPLIT SITE
DRIFTING
STRATEGIES
THEORIES
what's happening?
CHILD'S VOICE
ORGANISATIONAL FACTORS
HELP?
HINDER?
NEXT STEPS
Support for Mum
CHANGE + AUTISM
SEN Dept
Stepfather's absence
SIZE of SCHOOL

GROUND RULES
ALTERNATIVE EDUCATIONAL PROVISION
LIVING with FRIENDS
EXPLORING RELATIONSHIP
PROBLEM Presenter
LATE!
Year 9 GIRL
CIRCLE of ADULTS
"MUM"
WARMTH
LIKE A PARENT
LINDA
INNOVATE
Y8
RESPECT
DEPRESSION
STRATEGIES
HYPOTHESSS
SYSTEM/ORGANISATIONAL FAC
Helped by
Hindered by
Yearning for parent figure
Terrified of all kinds of things
Fear of growing up
Contracts
Small groups

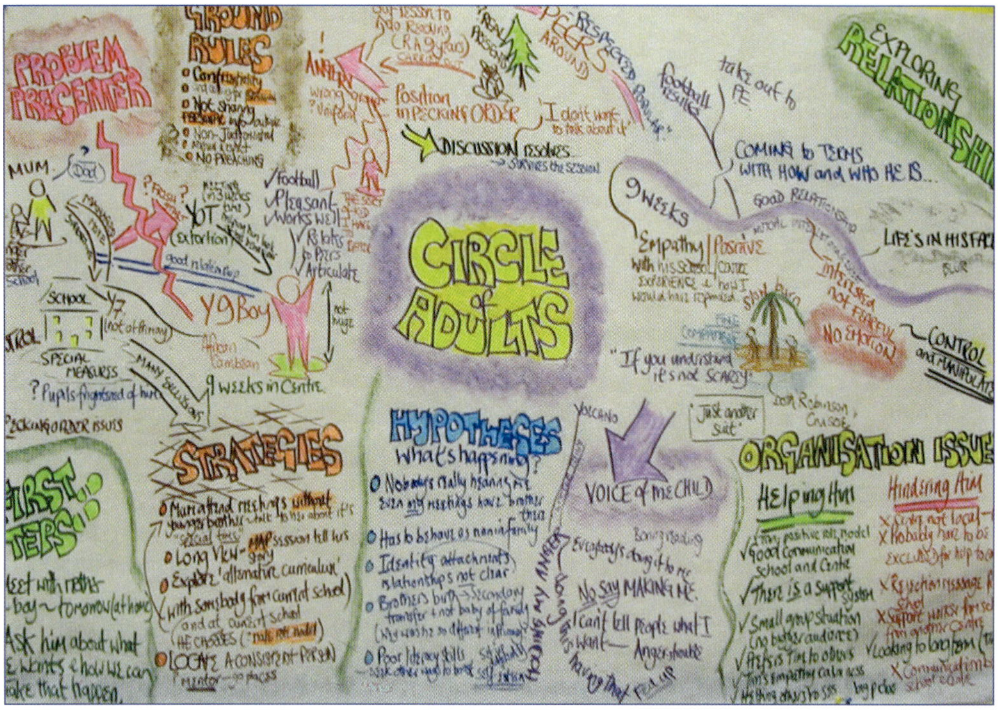
PROBLEM PRESENTER
GROUND RULES
PEERS
EXPLORING RELATIONSHIPS
CIRCLE of ADULTS
Y9 Boy
9 weeks in Centre.
STRATEGIES
HYPOTHESES
What's happening?
VOICE of the CHILD
ORGANISATION ISSUES
Helping Him
Hindering Him
FIRST STEPS
"If you understand it's not SCARY"
CONTROL and MANIPULATE
NO EMOTION

LISTEN TO EACH OTHER
OPENNESS TO NEW IDEAS
SPEAK IN FIRST PERSON
NO JUDGING
CONFIDENTIAL
"TALK TIME"
SABOTAGE the GROUP
ANGRY with ADULTS
FEMALE STAFF
RELATIONSHIP
TALKED FOR 3 hours.
WEEKLY VISIT.
CIRCLE of ADULTS
1:1 Context
TRUST
talk ~ SENSITIVE to other's NEEDS
HYPOTHESES
What's happening
STRATEGIES
VOICE of the CHILD
My dream is to be a fantastic chef
FIRST STEPS
ORGANISATIONAL FACTORS
Help
Hinder
'FANTASTIC'
PRU.
8 years
Older brothers
CARER

THE 10 STEPS

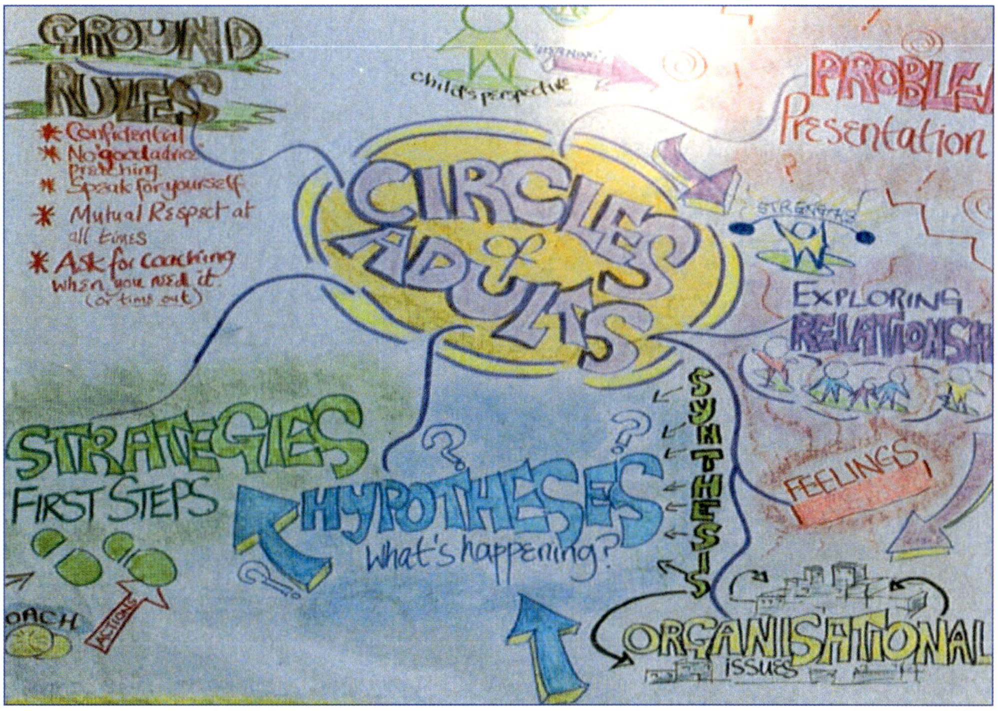

Once the preparatory stages have been agreed and completed, the 10 key stages of the Circle of Adults process are as follows:

1. Agree GROUND RULES for the session to come

2. PRESENT PROBLEM

3. EXPLORE RELATIONSHIPS

4. Consider ORGANISATIONAL FACTORS that help or hinder the problem situation

5. Listen to what the CHILD'S VOICE has to say

6. Listen to a SYNTHESIS of all that have been recorded so far

7. Generate HYPOTHESES that help make sense of what is happening

8. Generate STRATEGIES linked to the hypotheses

9. Agree some FIRST STEPS the problem presenter can take in the very near future and appoint a coach to check these have been accomplished by an agreed time

10. The session closes with a summary comment from each participant - a 'Round of Words'

STEP 1
Ground Rules
Suggested time for this step
5 minutes

Effective group work requires clear boundaries and one way of providing these is to agree the ground rules. Ground rules are there to enhance feelings of safety within the group. Groups can usually create their own rules and this helps their ownership of the process. However, the outline rules that follow have worked well in our experience and if any are not spontaneously proposed by the group they are worth prompting or suggesting as useful additions:

- Speak from your own experience. 'Own' your statements, e.g. 'I believe', 'I think'.
- Don't give 'good advice'/don't preach.
- Give feedback to other group members that is owned, specific and balanced. Speak for yourself and of your own experiences in detailed and precise terms, providing both positives and negatives in balance. For instance: 'For me, my feelings about Paul are that he can be both likeable and totally infuriating.'
- Maintain confidentiality regarding all personal material discussed in the session unless agreed otherwise. Don't discuss outside group unless clearly in interests of those concerned.

As the 'rules' emerge these should be recorded on the graphic; it is usually worth numbering them for easy reference. There should be just enough discussion of the rules to ensure a reasonable level of consensus - everybody is able to say they can live with all of the rules. Sometimes it is worth asking the group which of the rules are essential to establish a sufficient level of trust within the group for the session which is about to follow. Remind the group that they have now given you, the facilitators, permission to police their adherence to the ground rules, and that you will indeed be listening for any breaches and will challenge these. To strengthen this further - ask the group <u>how</u> they would like to be challenged if they break a rule - a word? A sign? Eye contact? This can be done in a light hearted way but serves to remind the group that there is no point in having rules unless something happens when they are broken! *

A Word on Seating Layout

The best arrangement is for the group to sit in a semi-circle around the graphic so all can see the developing picture. The process facilitator should encourage participants to speak to the centre of the group, not to each other. In doing this, you're trying to create a pool of common meaning, not a set of person-to-person dynamics.

Footnote:
*For more great ideas on setting the tone in meetings and policing ground rules see: 'Making Meetings Matter' by Marsha Forest and Jack Pearpoint. Inclusion Press 1997 www.inclusion.com

STEP 2

Present Problem

Suggested time for this step
15 minutes

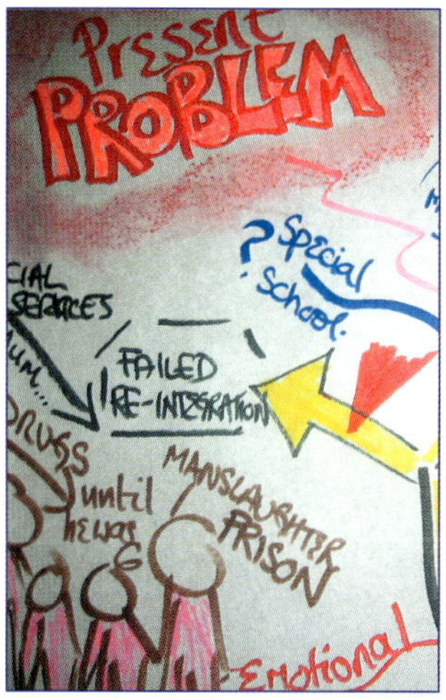

The essence of this step is that the problem presenter is given up to 15 minutes to describe all that they think relevant about the young person under consideration. The process facilitator pretty much lets the problem presenter talk without interruption during this Step. The graphic recorder keeps a record of key words and images as these emerge and the process facilitator supports the problem presenter in telling his or her story. The rest of the group listens.

Towards the end of the 15 minutes the process facilitator may want to ask the group if the young person is known to anyone else and whether they have anything they want to add to what has been said so far. Group members may ask for any factual points to be clarified in what they have heard so far. Do not allow group members to advance theories or hypotheses during this Step - if this happens, ask the group member to hold onto that thought as it will be needed when we come to Step 7.

During Step 2 the process facilitator should discourage any extended 'discussion' of what the problem presenter has told the group - there isn't time - it is seldom, if ever, productive and, even worse, risks the group going off at a tangent with one voice dominating. Keep to the boundaries between Steps! In general, there is no going back to revisit earlier steps, and although a bit of information felt to be crucial by the problem presenter could be added at a later stage, this would be an exception. Remember, as the facilitators, you must finish on time - having completed all the Steps. Failure to do this simply invites disappointment and frustration.

Assuming the issues so far described around the young person are messy, complex and undermining of the current school placement (and they should be if you are investing time in the Circle of Adults process!) then there is likely to be a palpable dip in the group's energy level at this point as individual members become concerned that the issues might be intractable and/or beyond their power to influence. Good facilitation acknowledges this dip as a sign that the difficulties have been looked at squarely. It is also useful for one of the facilitators to note that the usual next step in our problem solving is to go straight to working out strategies to solve the difficulties. We like to name this as a 'premature leap to solutions' and note that there is still much more we need to hear about the young person and his or her situation. In fact there are 4 further steps to go through in Circle of Adults before we will begin to look at strategies.

> **"Sometimes clarity of insight is only possible because of the lack of detail."**
>
> Harrison Owen 2002

STEP 3

Explore Relationships

Suggested time for this step 15 minutes

Step 3 sees the process facilitator pose a range of open-ended guiding questions to the problem presenter. Each question aims to help the problem presenter describe the quality of their relationship with the young person in question.

What is implied here is that we can learn from the feelings that a young person produces in us, tap into our natural human capacity to resonate to others' emotional states and recognise that this gives us a clue to how they might be feeling.

The Circle of Adults process uses the following leading questions to open this area up:

- It asks the problem presenter to describe the history of his/her relationship with the child, particularly their first meeting with the young person.
- It asks the problem presenter to tell us what a 'fly on the wall' describing the relationship would tell us.
- It asks the problem presenter to imagine they were alone on a desert island with the young person - how would that be?
- It asks the problem presenter if the young person reminds them of anyone past or present. The process facilitator should also ask the group as a whole whether the young person reminds them of anyone they have worked with or known in the past. If someone is reminded of another young person, then they should be encouraged to tell what the longer-term outcomes were for that person. Sometimes this invitation results in the telling of a story that turns out more hopefully than expected. Sometimes it doesn't.

Step 3 is about the metaphors, feelings and hunches that rise to the surface when we are trying to make complex judgements or process a lot of possibly contradictory information. The imaginary situations - the fly on the wall, the desert island - are deliberately light hearted - and function as 'props' that give permission to the problem presenter to safely communicate emotion. The process facilitator needs to take particular care within this Step not to indulge in any interpretation of what the problem presenter says in answer to the leading questions. Nor should any member of the group be allowed to do this.
The problem presenter has not signed up for 'therapy' or a searching examination of their deeper motives and they will quickly withdraw if they feel the process is moving in this direction.

"The end is in the beginning"

Bruno Bettelheim 1993

As the process facilitator moves the group into Step 4, all of the group become actively involved in the process and will continue to be so until the close. The spotlight moves from its focus on the problem presenter and the facilitators now begin to engage the problem solving capacity of all the members. The graphic recorder keeps a record in two separate columns of the factors that the group feels are either helping or hindering the problem presented.

STEP 4

Organisational / Systemic Factors

Suggested time for this step
10 minutes

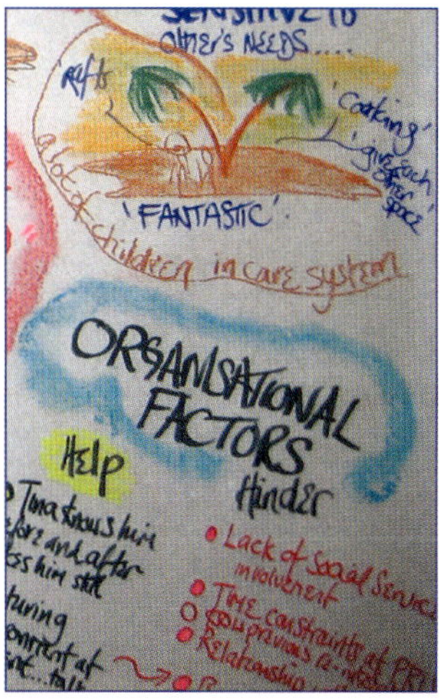

There are two main aims for the facilitators to keep at the front of their minds during this Step.

First - *To strengthen the problem presenter.*
This is an opportunity for the group to name and highlight what they have noticed about the positive contributions, skills and expertise of the problem presenter. Any opportunity to have the problem presenter's strengths recognised and acknowledged should be seized by the facilitators (and not just during this Step). It is almost a truism, within the UK educational world at least, that frontline staff typically underestimate their power to make a difference to individual students - so anything that counters this tendency is likely to be worth doing. It is perfectly OK for either of the facilitators to set the ball rolling here and go first in naming what they have appreciated about the way the problem presenter has dealt with issues so far. These should be listed under the 'Factors which Help' section of the graphic.

Second - *To look at the bigger system picture.*
This Step is also an opportunity to name and highlight system and organisational factors that are perceived by the group to be either helping or hindering a resolution of the presented problem. It is especially useful for the group to name any system/organisational factors that they feel make life more difficult for the problem presenter

10 minutes is usually more than enough for Step 4; don't let the group get bogged down in too many system factors that are felt to hinder the situation - aim for a roughly equal sized 'Helps' and 'Hinders' lists. It is likely that the graphic recorder will want to call time on this Step as he or she begins to run out of available space on the graphic. As for all the Steps - be careful as facilitators that you don't lose momentum by dwelling too long in one space - one of the reasons the Circle of Adults process is effective is that it constantly pushes forward.

STEP 5

Listen to the 'Child's Voice'

Suggested time for this step
2 minutes

The facilitators need to find a volunteer to provide the group with the voice of the child at the start of the process - usually just before they embark on Step 2.

Very little coaching or prompting is given to the group member who undertakes to listen to Steps 2, 3 and 4 with the child or young person's perspective in mind. Enlisting a volunteer with a light-hearted question like; 'Who can easily get in touch with their 10 year-old* self?' is usually successful. Matching the group member and the child's gender doesn't seem to matter too much here. Go with whoever volunteers - even if you are not sure they seem right for the role - we have often been surprised.

As Step 5 is reached the process facilitator invites the individual to tell the group what they think the young person would say about himself or herself if they were here with us - "So Darren what are you feeling?" This is often a key moment in the Circle of Adults session. It invites an intuitive and empathic insight from the adult who has taken this role and is best delivered in the first person (most volunteers do this instinctively - but if they don't then this should be prompted)
The 'child's voice' is received with little or no comment from the facilitators - a short monologue is best. If you judge the child's voice volunteer to be particularly fluent then it can be worth asking the 'child' a few guiding questions - Very open ended ones work best: When are things at their best for you? What would your dream for the future be?

One or more group members may be moved to tears whilst listening to the child's voice. Expect this and recognise it as a sign that some true connection is being made.

Resist any temptation to move into problem solving or interrogatory mode - the child's voice is very likely to be an emotionally rich part of the process but we are not doing a full-blown psychodrama here. The rule - 'Less is More' serves this step well.

The process facilitator closes this Step by checking back briefly with the problem presenter - 'Does that fit?' ' Does that make sense for you?' - you are not inviting a discussion of what has just been said or a detailed commentary, you are simply seeking an affirmation.

"I am a human being; therefore nothing human is alien to me"

Terence Afer (c. 190-158 B.C.)

Footnote:

*Use the actual age of the child who is the focus of the session.

STEP 6

The Synthesis

Suggested time for this step
2/3 minutes

This step is taken by the graphic facilitator who has been listening to the developing story and in particular for those bits of the narrative that don't necessarily make sense on first hearing. As the next step in the process will be 'Hypotheses' it is helpful to introduce the Synthesis as alerting the group 'to those parts of the story that a good hypothesis should enable us to understand'.

Step 6 is relatively brief (no more than 2/3 minutes) and is processed by the graphic facilitator. Graphic facilitation is primarily about listening and up to this point, part of the graphic facilitator's attention has been on those parts of the story so far that are hard to make sense of, don't fit with other parts of the story or on seeming omissions in the story. It is these kinds of thoughts that are fed back to the group during the Synthesis. Providing a useful Synthesis for the group relies on the ability of the graphic facilitator to be able to 'stand aside' from the blow by blow content of what has been said by the group up to that point. This is not easy. Even the best facilitators get sucked into the story at times and lose focus on the underlying issues or paradoxes that lurk below the surface content. Importantly, the Synthesis is not a summary of what is recorded so far on the graphic paper. More than that, you are searching for the linkages and patterns in what you have heard. Listen for the key images, the strong feelings (particularly from the 'Child's Voice') as they have arisen. It is often worth introducing the Synthesis with the idea that you are going to point out some conflicting or confusing aspects of the story that 'a good theory will help us make sense of...' For example, it is sometimes part of a problem presentation that the young person comes across as being very negative about almost all aspects of school and seems to find nothing rewarding in their school day but has 100% attendance. A good theory would help us make sense of these two seemingly conflicting descriptions of how this child is being understood. It is the graphic facilitator's job to notice these contradictory parts of the narrative and lay them in front of the group for consideration.

STEP 7

Generate Hypotheses

Suggested time for this step
10 minutes

The Circle of Adults session becomes much pacier at this point. Encourage the group to suggest as many different theories/hypotheses as they can generate in the few minutes that are allowed for this step. The facilitators should remind the group that this is a time for 'Yes and…' and not 'Yes but…' meaning that, where possible, participants should build on each other's hypotheses not attempt to refute or disagree with them - there is no time for argument or discussion.

Nor is there any pressure on individuals to make their hypothesis consistent with any of the other hypotheses. Step 7 is genuinely eclectic and the facilitators should encourage the group to give voice to as many different perspectives/theoretical accounts as they can manage. Facilitation needs to be quite tight and 'pushy' during this Step. Group members may come up with a contribution or a question that attempts to revisit an earlier Step in some way. Do not allow this, there isn't time and the whole process will lose impetus if the facilitators let sidebar discussions develop outside of the content they are requesting within this Step. If a seemingly irrelevant comment is made, simply ask the group member: "and your theory is...?" If they haven't got one - move on to someone who has.

Assuming you have a 'No Preaching' ground rule in force for the session, you may need to be vigilant that this rule is not breached during Step 7. Encourage the group to be tentative as they give their hypotheses. It's about what *might* be happening with the young person in question.

It is often useful within this Step to remind the group of some of the hard to understand issues that were uncovered within the 'Synthesis' and encourage hypotheses that attempt to account for these.

STEP 8

Generate Strategies

Suggested time for this step 10 minutes

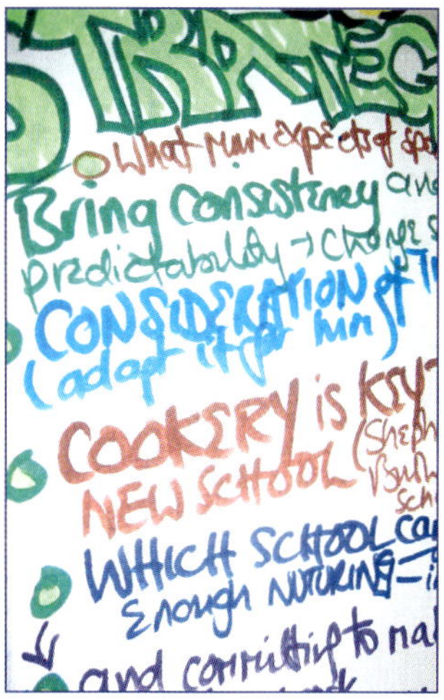

In introducing this Step the facilitators should make it clear that they are looking for strategies that have clear links to the hypotheses generated in Step 7. Too often participants in 'problem solving discussions' wheel out their 'usual suspects' at this point in the proceedings, 'star charts', 'counselling' 'mentoring' and the rest. Any or all of these strategies might be helpful to the child being thought about, but the facilitators need to push the group to elaborate and clarify the links between their suggested strategies and the understandings that have been arrived at in the previous 7 steps of the process.

Continually encourage the group to add to, elaborate on and strengthen each other's suggested strategies. The problem presenter needs to be a quiet listener during this step and the facilitators need to take care not to let him/her interrupt or undermine the strategy building process by saying 'Tried that - didn't work' about any particular idea suggested. Simply remind the presenter that at the conclusion of this step they will have their choice of the ideas they think hold some promise for them and that they will be invited to design some first steps around those ideas.

It can often be helpful (assuming you are facilitating in a school/educational setting) in this Step to direct the group's thinking towards what Gerda Hanko has called "the therapeutic potential in the day-to-day curriculum" (Hanko 1999) and push for explicit links between the child's perceived needs and the curriculum.

"For it is important that awake people be awake,
Or a breaking line may discourage them back to sleep;
The signals we give - yes or no, or maybe -
Should be clear: the darkness around us is deep."

William Stafford: A Ritual To Read To Each Other

STEP 9

Agree First Steps

Suggested time for this step
5 minutes

The problem presenter is invited to identify two or three of the strategies suggested in Step 9 that look as if they could be promising and to figure out a very specific first step for each. The facilitators need to be ruthless in pushing the problem presenter to decide on a concrete action outcome associated with the strategy - do not accept vague indications or expressions of good intent*, what you need here are clear commitments to do things by a certain agreed time. First steps can be small - a phone call, arranging a meeting, sharing the content of the Circle of Adults session with a key person who was not at the meeting. But they need to be done soon. We are interested in what the problem presenter can commit to doing tomorrow, by the end of the week or by this time next week. The chances of the problem presenter actually doing something are further increased if they can be encouraged to take their first step together with someone else and be invited to name that person there and then. At the very least it is always worth asking the problem presenter to nominate someone in the Circle of Adults group whose job it will be to check on whether they have done what they said they would do in the time specified.

Footnote:

Whilst resolutions such as 'Listen to the child more' or 'Take time to talk to the child's parents' may be full of heart-warming good intentions, they are not clear and realisable first steps of the sort we are pushing for in Step 10. Much better would be: "Tomorrow I will fix a date (within the next week) to meet individually with the child and get their view on what goes well for them at school" or "Tomorrow I will talk to our Senco, and agree a date for us to meet with the child's parents and get their perspective on what helps their child stay on track with their behaviour"

STEP 10

The Closing Round of Words

Suggested time for this step no more than 3 minutes

The closing 'round of words' is designed to validate each person's experience of the session by inviting their summary comment - in no more than 3 or 4 words. The aim is closure and this is not a time for speeches or to re-open any parts of the process that may remain unresolved. The facilitators need to make this clear to participants before beginning the round.

In all of the Circle of Adult's sessions we have run to date, the problem presenter has usually been the final person to speak. But at the end of a very recent session a participant expressed surprise that we didn't give the last word to the 'child' - that was an unarguable point and seemed to us to be totally in tune with the spirit of this work. So that is what we now do.

FREQUENTLY ASKED QUESTIONS

1. Who would you use this approach with?

The approach works well with the following participants:

- Multi agency teams involved in complex and high profile casework.
- Staff groups gathered together on a voluntary basis with the aim of improving understandings and developing strategies around the most challenging pupils attending their school.
- Formal pastoral meetings that involve key stakeholders in school or other setting e.g. tutor, head of year and involved subject staff in a secondary school, or class teacher, Teaching Assistant, SENCO and Headteacher in a primary, with involved outside agencies also invited.
- Professional development/staff support groups in a range of settings.

2. How many people can be present?

A group size of about 8-12 works best and ensures good levels of participation by all. With larger groups consider option of an inner circle of about 8-10 key individuals and a 'silent' outer circle who you involve only at the 'Hypotheses' and the 'Strategies' stages of the process.

3. Does it work?

It appears clear from evaluation work undertaken so far that participants in the Circle of Adults process and in comparable teacher support groups report that they feel supported, have an improved understanding of the young person and that these outcomes in turn lead to more effective choices of strategies for individual pupils. In a study of primary teachers, Nias et al (1989) found those schools that had a professionally and emotionally supportive staff were also the most effective in being supportive towards their pupils. Those who wish to read further around the value and efficacy of working with teacher and multi agency groups are directed to: Hanko (1985, 1999), Stringer et al (1992), Newton (1995), Gill and Monsen (1995, 1996), Stockley (2003) and Farouk (2004).

4. What if somebody cries?

Tears can unnerve the most experienced facilitators. What do we do? Where are the tissues? Tears are to be expected; the process is an emotive one, and it is worth mentioning this at the very start of the session so that there are no surprises. Participants can be encouraged to make whatever accommodations they need to if they are moved to emotion including; leaving the room for a short break, crying on the shoulder of the person next to them (with their permission!) or simply taking a moment of quiet. It is worth emphasising that participants need to take responsibility for managing their feelings and that you do not have a range of counsellors lined up outside the door! This is not an individual therapy session (although individuals may well find it therapeutic). If the focus person is moved to tears, there are a range of helpful questions the facilitator can ask including; 'What are these tears telling us?' 'What do the tears mean for you?' 'Can you put words to these tears?' It is important to acknowledge, permit and recognise emotional expressions without judgement and equally, it is important not to ignore them.

5. What if it looks impossible?

At times it will feel impossible! How can you possibly bring home an entrenched and stuck situation? The answer is simple; trust the process! Very often we have endured feelings of near panic, 'stuckness' and a dread that there will be nowhere positive to go - particularly in the early steps of the process. By the end of the process we too have often been amazed at what has actually emerged from the session in terms of insights, strategies and doable first steps.

6. What do you do if the meeting starts to break down into conflict?

Keep calm! Breathe, go to the balcony, look at the view, think what you will do and say, return and act! Or, more simply, in the words of Jack Pearpoint and Marsha Forrest: ' Breathe, Think, Act!' Conflict pre-emption is always the best strategy and by following the discipline of the processes described above, difficulties should be minimised. However if things do erupt, calmly remind the group of the ground rules or process boundaries. Assert the need to listen to each other respectfully without having to fully agree with each other. People are entitled to a point of view. Inclusive practice is about constructive coexistence, not everyone loving each other all the time. Look for opportunities to build a consensus in which those in the room can live with the way forward, hypotheses or strategies, rather than having to be completely in agreement with every part of them. And remember that the final selection of strategies and first steps is the responsibility of the problem presenter - no one else.

7. Everyone goes silent. What do you do?

Often, you can simply live with the silence and use it to give people time to think. Too often we can be tempted to rush in and fill silences unnecessarily. At other times silences can be used to recap what has been said by using the wall graphic summary so far.

> **"Silences are okay - they can be working silences.."**
>
> Carl Rogers quoted in Lynn Hoffman's 'Family Therapy - An Intimate Journey'

8. I don't have anyone to co-facilitate with - can I run the session by myself?

In short - no, you can't, and if you try, you will very quickly find yourself falling behind with the graphic and/or losing touch with your process facilitation. Remember the Circle of Adults process is designed to be co-facilitated and the assumption is that steering the group to some constructive outcomes for the child in question is more than one person's work. Co-facilitation also provides a vital safety net for each of the facilitators and means that if one facilitator finds themselves hopelessly off-track or sucked into the content or involved in a power struggle with a group member then the likelihood is that the other facilitator will spot this and intervene to put the process back on track. Don't do it alone!

9. OK - So how do I learn to do this?

As should be clear by now, the facilitation tool described in this book involves co-facilitation of group planning and problem solving. This is not a tool for the solo player. It is not enough to read about Circle of Adults and then go and carry out the process with a group. A period of practice with others who also want to learn the tool's use is essential and could be built around the following activities:

- Establish a group of like-minded learners with at least 6-8 members all of whom want to learn to use Circle of Adults and are able to commit to 'staying the course' by meeting together over an extended period. Meetings will typically last for up to 3 hours and there will need to be as many meetings as there are members in the group.

- A regular series of meetings, probably monthly, in which members of the group take it in turns to be the subject of what is being practised. This aspect of learning about the use of person centred planning tools is non-negotiable and is fundamental to the values that underpin this work. We should not expect those we serve to undergo processes that we ourselves have no experience of and, equally importantly, there is no more immediate learning experience than being in the process as yourself. Ever after you will be a more careful and empathic facilitator because you will be able to touch back to that time when you were in the 'hot seat' and your memories of how that felt. Group members also need to take turns in the different facilitation roles and receive feedback -their own and others-on their performance.

- Where possible the group should enlist coaching from facilitators who are already experienced in the use of Circle of Adults or other person centred planning tools. If this is not possible then another point of reference is the various video and written teaching materials obtainable from the Inclusive Solutions web site: www.inclusive-solutions.com

10. I want to tell them what to do!

Beware of giving your best ideas whilst facilitating. Because you are leading the session there are already great risks of being looked to as the 'expert'. If you are sitting on what you think is an amazing or important insight or strategy the only way you can feed this in is by turning your idea into a question or using the idea as you shape up the hypotheses and strategies of other group members. But beware and tread very carefully! Step out of the facilitator's role at your peril!

11. There are so many issues around the child I want to run the 'Circle of Adults' session for - I don't think we can do it all justice in an hour and a half - what should I do?

You're right - you likely can't cover everything in one session! This doesn't mean you can't do anything. If you start with the belief that there is more we can understand about the child you want to run the session for, then whatever is achieved in the time available will be worthwhile. You don't have to solve everything in one burst. Indeed it is likely group members will benefit from the chance to reflect on any new insights gained in the session. You can always come back and think together again.

12. Should I be inviting the young person's parents/carers to the Circle of Adults session?

Good question! So far our answer has been 'No' and the rationale has been as follows:

We have wondered whether parents'/carers' presence would inevitably inhibit the group's explorations of family relationships and lead to people censoring their contributions for fear of upsetting or offending family members. We have reaffirmed that the process is not about providing direct family support but confirmed that it is about providing direct support to the child's front line worker. And no doubt you can think up your own reasons why you wouldn't invite family to the session.

But it is also easy to have doubts about any of the above rationalisations - not least that they all underscore the conspiracy of silence that much of our professional work rests on. Just how visible do we think our work should be?

There are some very clear precedents for including parents/carers in this sort of work - most notably the work of Tom Andersen and his family therapy team in Norway (see 'The Reflecting Team' Andersen 1991)

So, at the time of writing this we have not yet run a Circle of Adults session with parents/carers present. We are actively considering how we could do this and what (if any) changes to the process would be needed to keep the session productive and safe for all. Watch this space!

WORKED EXAMPLE

What follows is an account of a Circle of Adults session run with a group of 30+ middle and high school managers (head teachers, deputies, year managers, heads of support units and Sencos) from an English Education Authority. Names and some identifying details have been changed to preserve anonymity. Our commentary on the process is in italics and follows the descriptions of each Step. The problem presenter - Mr Black - was the head of year 8 in a middle school and the form tutor for the young person concerned. Also in the group was member of staff - Fiona - from the same school. She also knew the young person well. During the course of the session it emerged that the teacher with responsibility for 'behaviour' at the high school the young person was due to transfer to in the coming school year was also part of the group - so some impromptu transition planning was a part of what follows.

STEP 1 - Ground Rules

The following ground rules were proposed and agreed by the group:

Respect the confidentiality of this session
Take it in turns to speak
No preaching
Keep positive
A no blame culture should be in force
No confrontations
Take the time you need

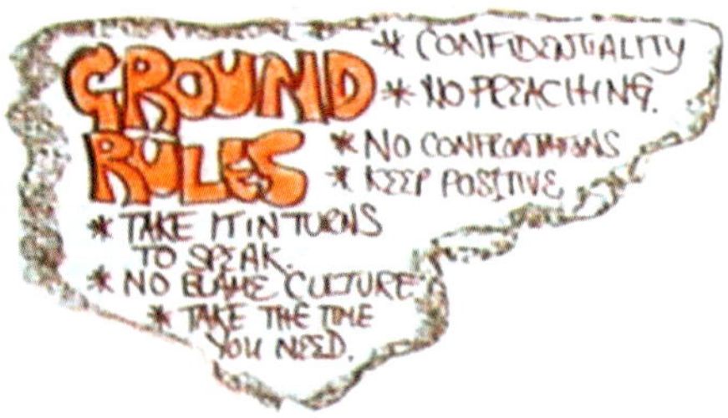

Commentary:

There were probably more ground rules than we would have liked here - 7 separate rules could be a lot to police from the facilitators' point of view! But this was a group who had never worked together in this way before so maybe they felt the need to build in as much safety/protection as they could up front. The final rule - 'take the time you need' - is interesting; the person proposing it said she wondered if strong feelings might surface in the discussion and, if so, didn't want anyone to feel rushed.

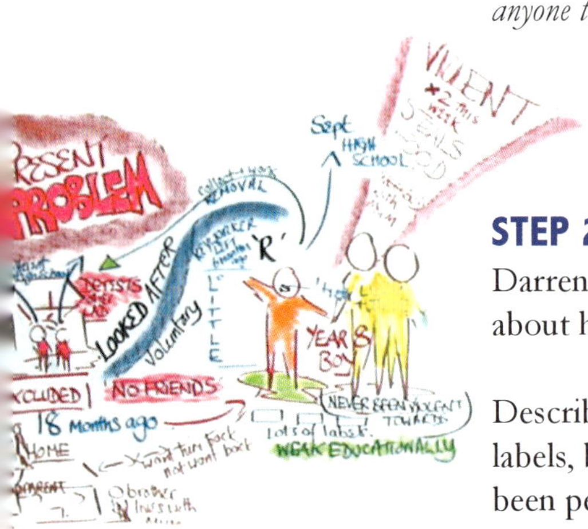

STEP 2 - Present Problem

Darren was a year 8 pupil, small for his age; the first thing you were likely to notice about him was his very badly cared for teeth.

Described as 'weak educationally', Darren had also been given lots of special needs labels, but the problem presenter (Mr Black) didn't elaborate on these. Darren had been permanently excluded from at least one other school in the past. He had been on roll at his current school for 18 months and there had been no exclusions from here to date. Thus the 'problem' for Mr Black did not centre on managing Darren's behaviour at present. There were challenging episodes to deal with day by day (violence towards other children, stealing food) but Mr Black clearly felt in control of and able to contain Darren. He had used a number of successful strategies with Darren including putting him in a mentoring role with younger students. The main concern in Mr Black's mind was that Darren was due to transfer to High School in about two months time. Mr Black viewed this transfer with foreboding and could readily anticipate early exclusions from the new setting given what he knew about Darren's capacity for provoking confrontations with other students (particularly ones much bigger than himself!).

Mr Black described how he had learnt to read the signs that Darren was likely to become provocative and ultimately violent - he knew some but not all of the things that triggered these episodes. A particular recent trigger had been when Darren had spent a weekend with his mother in the family home.

In amongst this, Mr Black made a point of saying that Darren had never been violent towards any staff member.

Mr Black could readily find positives and strengths in Darren. He described him as often 'incredibly caring' towards others and told the group how he had enlisted Darren to help younger pupils with their reading and how he had even taken Darren on a school trip as a kind of unofficial helper with those same younger pupils. Mr Black summed up Darren at his best by saying that 'on a good day he can be the chirpiest lad in the school'

However Mr Black also said that Darren had no friends within his year group and that other pupils were generally wary of him or actively disliked him.
Mr Black had a lot to tell the group about Darren's family situation and life outside of school. Darren was currently in 'voluntary care' and had been in and out of care settings for a number of years. His mother's relationship with him was described as 'ambivalent at best' with periods where she seemed to want him back with her and periods where she did not want him in the family home. At other times Darren had lived briefly with a step-grandparent. Darren's younger stepbrother had, however, lived continuously in with his mother. No mention was made of Darren's father.

Darren was described as having an especially volatile relationship with another young person in his current care home - Wayne. Mr Black said Darren 'detests the lad' and staff there had huge difficulties in containing the worst of this relationship. One key worker in the care home had had some success in managing this conflict, but she had recently left. Happily, Wayne and Darren were due to attend different high schools but in Darren's case this would also involve a move of care home. This added to Mr Black's worries about the stability of Darren's future school placement as he attributed some of his success with Darren to the good communications he had established with staff at the care home.

In summary, Mr Black said his urgent concerns were: Firstly, how to avoid Darren's behaviour escalating in the last few weeks of term. His fear was that this would lead to him being permanently excluded before the end of the school year. And secondly, what, if anything, he could do to enable Darren to cope in his new school in September.

Commentary:

This was a full and thoughtful summary of the 'problem' by Mr Black. Key points were made with economy. It was clearly the story of a teacher who had forged a positive relationship with a young person that many others had found too hard to handle.

However, Mr Black's despair about the future was palpable and, by the end of this Step, he seemed to feel quite powerless to do anything that might positively influence the remainder of Darren's school career. It was as if he felt that all he had achieved with Darren was going to count for nothing.

STEP 3 - Explore Relationship

Mr Black's earliest memory of Darren within school was of a cheery pupil who always said 'Hello', but he remembered that even then he could see - writ large - Darren's 'self destruct button'. At that point Mr Black is simply Darren's Head of Year and mostly in the role of 'trouble-shooter'.

Over time Darren had become part of Mr Black's tutor group and came more directly under what Mr Black then described as his 'care'. It was becoming more and more apparent to Mr Black that Darren seemed very 'detached from his feelings' and any questions about these would typically be met with a shrug.

As an example of how he had attempted to work around Darren's reluctance to discuss feelings, Mr Black described a strategy involving what he called 'The Secret Lunchbox'. The narrative was so compelling and insightful that we have reproduced it in detail (see page 48).

Mr Black said he quickly learned that Darren was the kind of pupil who, 'if he thinks you care - he would do anything for you'.

Darren was also someone who could just 'wander off' from any situation unless there was someone watching over him.

When asked if Darren reminded him of anyone Mr Black came up with the character 'Brick Pollitt' in Tennessee Williams' play 'Cat on a Hot Tin Roof' - someone who, unable to respond to other's pleas for communication, resorts to a self-destructive escape in alcohol.

Asked to imagine how it would be if here were marooned on a desert island with Darren, Mr Black had no hesitation in saying that he and Darren would become 'very close' that there would be laughter and of course 'Food'. 'Accidents' would also happen.

Towards the end of this step Mr Black voiced the insight that he, for Darren, was like 'The Dream of a Father'. The phrase hung in the air for some time and seemed full of meanings. Eventually the process facilitator asked Mr Black what he had done with this realisation. Mr Black said he'd felt he'd 'had to ignore it'.

Commentary:

You can only read the content of this step as it flows. No attempt should be made to logically connect pieces or to try and interpret or explain. Hunches, intuitions and metaphor are the currency of Step 3 and this is a fine example of what it the content should be if the step is fully realised. What stands out from the fuller story gathered in this step is that Darren has healthy, loveable parts of himself that were still reachable - if they had just heard the 'case history/episodes of difficulty/labels' description of Darren (i.e. Step 1 only) the group would not have known this.

STEP 4 - Organisational Factors

Factors felt by the group to be helping were as follows:

- Our consistency each morning in how we organise and approach things with Darren. (this was contributed by the problem presenter)
- The 'secret lunchbox' strategy and what this said about Mr Black's thoughtfulness in dealing with Darren.
- Mr Black's respectful relationship with Darren.
- Fiona's good relationship with Darren.
- The general tone of nurturing that characterises Mr Black's relationship with Darren.

Factors felt to be hindering were:

- Darren's relationships with certain learning support assistants in his current school.
- The fact that there was no consistent social services key worker for Darren.
- The fact that Darren has to sit in the classroom for long unstructured periods.
- Darren's impending transfer of school in September coming and the impending change of care home.
- The impersonal expectations of many schools their 'deficit cultures' especially as young people move up through the phases.

Commentary:

This was an ideal opportunity for the group to celebrate and amplify what they had appreciated about Mr Black's work with Darren to date. He could have been left in no doubt that the group were impressed by the quality of the relationship he had built with Darren. In the 'factors that hinder' list there are echoes of regret from the group that schools and other support services do not always mange to create and sustain this level of relationship with their most troubled students. There is also a growing sense of urgency in the group that events are about to come to a head for Darren and that there are real threats ahead. This reminder serves us well when we come to Steps 7 & 8.

STEP 5 - The Child's Voice

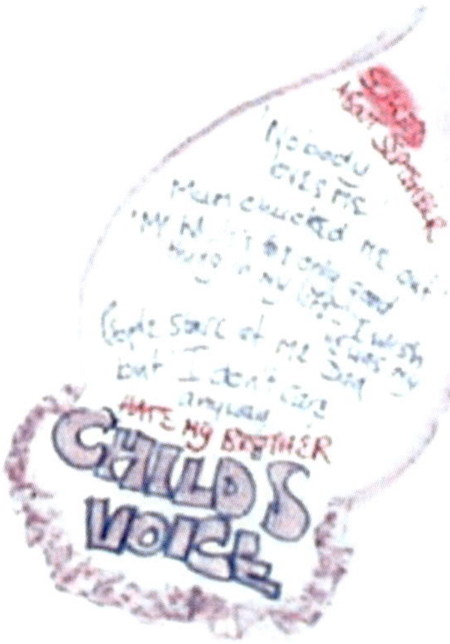

"I'm scared about September"

"Nobody loves me"

"Mr. Black's the only good thing in my life - I wish he was my Dad"

"My Mum chucked me out"

"People stare at me - but I don't care anyway"

"I hate my brother"

Commentary:

What is most striking about the content of this part of the process was that feelings words make their first appearance. Feelings of fear and hate are voiced as well as wishes and painful regrets. Very little in what had been said in Steps 1 - 4 had given the group any clues as to what Darren might be feeling in the midst of all the events around him and the changes that were on the horizon. The emotional content was high at this point in the process and there is no doubt several participants found that the content moved them.

Felt emotion within the group is a gift to the process and invariably makes for a more insightful session. Somehow it makes the group more able to 'think together' and thereby move beyond just 'discussing difficulties'.

STEP 6 - Synthesis

The graphic facilitator began the synthesis by reminding the group that this Step is not intended as a summary of what has been said so far. Rather it serves as a prelude to the next Step, 'Theories', by highlighting some aspects of the story so far that a good theory will help us make sense of, likely to be those parts of the story that don't quite 'fit' or that seem to 'jar'. This 'synthesis' directed the group's attention to the fact that the narrative right up to the 'Child's Voice' had been rather like a feelings-free zone. Despite an extended and thoughtful account of Darren's story we were still in the dark about what Darren himself was feeling - Why was this?

Secondly this synthesis directed the group's attention to the intense hostility within the relationship between Darren and Wayne and noticed that it was not yet clear what this was about. It was suggested that a good theory would help us understand better why this animosity ran so deep and had been so long lived.

Commentary:

The group is now about two-thirds of the way through their time together. The graphic is likewise two-thirds complete. The floor is about to be thrown open for their best theories and strategies to emerge. The synthesis serves as a final pause for reflection, a reminder to embrace the complexity of what they have just heard.

STEP 7 - Theories

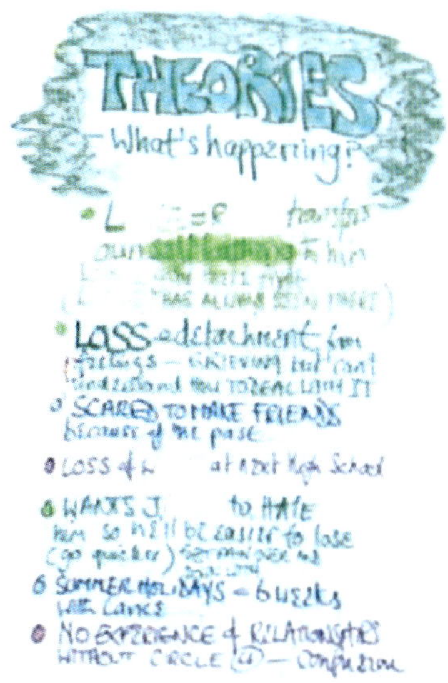

- Darren is scared to make friends because of his past experiences with peer relationships and their temporariness. Other voices in the group built on this theory by noting that almost all of the relationships Darren has at present were with people who were paid to be in his life.
- Darren is behaving like this because he wants Mr. Black to end up hating him - this will make it easier for Darren to get over the loss of this relationship.
- …and linked to this: To understand Darren you have to appreciate the big part that loss plays in his life, this has led him to become detached from his own feelings - the fact is that underneath the 'behaviour' he is grieving and doesn't know how to deal with the associated emotions.
- Wayne is a key figure in understanding Darren's behaviour. Wayne gets to go first to the places that Darren also ends up at - care home and school, Wayne has always been there in Darren's childhood and because of this Darren transfers his self-loathing to Wayne. Another participant added to this theory by noting that the summer holiday period was approaching and that this would mean 6 weeks in Wayne's company.

Commentary:

The group's thinking in this Step was of high quality and individuals readily built upon each other's contributions. Importantly, the issues raised within the 'Synthesis' received attention. The graphic facilitator was at full stretch just to keep up with the theories being advanced - always a sign that a session is going well!

STEP 8 - Strategies

These flowed from the group very quickly and were as follows:

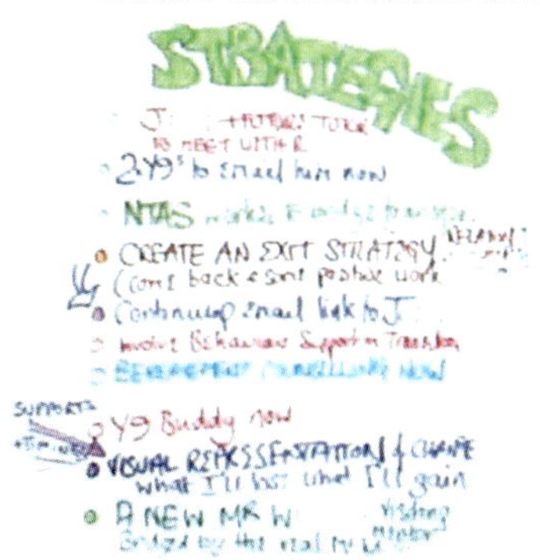

- Arrange a meeting between Darren, Mr Black and Darren's future year 9 tutor.
- Build links now with Darren's future school by arranging for a couple of their Year 9 students to email Darren as soon as possible.
- Find a non-teaching assistant or other worker immediately who can work to bridge Darren's school transfer.

- Locate a potential 'buddy' for Darren in the current year 9 of his future school.
- Provide a continuing email link between Mr Black and Darren.
- Create an 'Exit Strategy'.
- Involve the Behaviour Support Team in the transition planning.
- Create a visual/graphic representation of the impending change for Darren and include on it pictures of 'What I've lost' and 'What I'll gain'.
- Locate a 'new Mr Black' in the High School, have him be a visiting 'mentor' and build a relationship with him bridged by the original Mr Black.
- Arrange bereavement counselling now.
- Set up a restorative dialogue between Darren and Wayne.

Commentary:

As will be obvious, strategies tend to come through as seeds of ideas and always need shaping up in dialogue with the problem presenter. The energy of this group was very much directed to the urgent need to make good transition plans for Darren and Mr Black was quick to latch on to a couple of the ideas that caught his imagination as will be apparent in Step 9.

STEP 9 - Next Steps

Mr Black was clear that his actions needed to be about doing the best preparation he could to ease Darren's transition to High School. He named 3 next steps, all of which were to be done/started within the next few days.

- Share this graphic with the rest of the team and with senior management.
- Read/rehearse the script for a restorative intervention as a prelude to a session with Darren and Wayne.
- Create a visual representation of the future changes for Darren and include in this images of his past times at this school. To begin this representation Mr Black would arrange to stay late at school one evening this week to take digital pictures of 'everything around our school'.
- Mr Black also said he would talk with Darren's current care home to arrange to take pictures of this setting.
- Finally, and as a very immediate first step, Mr Black asked the facilitators if he could take away a piece of their graphics paper to use for the visual representation!

Commentary:

These are true 'first steps' in the sense that you or I could ring Mr Black in a week's time and ask him whether he'd taken them, how the photos turned out, what the team's reaction to the graphic was etc - and expect answers with detail, news of further developments and so on. Reflecting on the session afterwards, Mr Black said he would never have predicted the content of his 'Next Steps' at the beginning of the process. We take this as a sign of a productive session, as evidence that some new insights have been gained.

STEP 10 - Closing Round of Words

'I can see the full story now'

'Complex'

'I was thinking about a child I am working with - some of this will be really helpful for him'

'Appreciated not jumping to solutions too soon'

'Hopeful'

'At first I thought we weren't going to get anywhere - amazed at how much clearer it's become'

'Very supportive'

'Emotional and hard to hear at times'

'Something of a roller-coaster ride for me - I wish I'd had the chance to do this a year ago' (Mr Black)

Commentary:

This had been a rich session and the closing round of words reflects this. Some found it hard to put into words how they were feeling about the process at that moment and this is fairly typical of sessions that have emotional depth. Nevertheless, all are helped in their own thinking by hearing what others think. This is the underlying intention of the last step in the Circle of Adults process.

And all that then remained was for the graphic to be taken down, rolled up and given to the problem presenter.

THE SECRET LUNCHBOX

The following account was written by the Year Head who was the problem presenter in the previous Worked Example. It describes his strategy for dealing with episodes of persistent stealing by the young person who was the focus of this Circle of Adults session. He focuses on the underlying emotional needs that he believes are being expressed. His strategy is aimed at meeting these in a way that takes away the young person's need to steal.

"We had a problem in school with food going missing. Children were finding their lunchboxes were short of food each day when they went to them, and this was causing parents to contact me voicing their concerns. This is despite the fact that the lunch boxes are collected at the start of every day and taken to a safe place in big plastic boxes. It became apparent after a while that it was Darren stealing the chocolate items from each lunchbox, and his methods were quite sophisticated as he was avoiding detection on most occasions. Children were resenting this and Darren was becoming even more alienated from his peers.

At this particular time Darren was going through a very difficult time in his personal life. He was transferring from one children's home to another and finding the change tough. I was very aware of the need to maintain his relationships with all the other children in his class. Therefore I contacted the manager of his current care home to suggest an idea that we could put in place for him.

It was my belief that Darren was behaving this way for two reasons. One, I believed he wished to have some control over something in his life. He was achieving this by behaving in a way that enabled him to do something no other children would know about. Two, it was my view that Darren wanted the psychological benefits of eating to help him through this tricky period. What he was constantly eating was also very detrimental to Darren's weight problem.

To address both of the needs I believed that Darren had, I proposed to his children's home that we secreted a lunchbox in a place known to Darren in the school building. I would stock it every morning with cereal bars and raisins and fruit. Darren was then able to take the food from the lunchbox during the day. The one proviso was that nobody was allowed to find out what Darren was doing so he was not allowed to leave lessons. It had to be done in his own time.

Initially I stocked the box with 5/6 items a day, all of which were eaten. No more food was taken from other children's lunchboxes, which was a relief. After a week or so, I reduced the amount of food I stocked the box with until I was just putting in a box of raisins every day. These were still being taken most days until the system had been in place for around 4/5 weeks, when I stopped putting anything in it. Darren didn't mention it to me, and - touch wood - he has not stolen from any lunchboxes since. He fulfilled his need to behave in a sneaky way to give him control, and also got some grub. His relationship with the other children didn't suffer anymore either.

Consider how easy it would have been for the Year Head concerned to apply a behavioural perspective in an attempt to 'eradicate' the stealing. This would probably have involved confronting Darren about the stealing (and dealing with his likely denials), issuing a warning about the consequences if he continues and upping the level of sanction imposed when he does continue. Instead little is said directly to Darren and nothing is said about the stealing as such. There is a tacit acceptance of Darren's need for food at this particular time, but no confrontation or demands for change. The complete success of the 'secret lunchbox' strategy speaks for itself. Consider the value of this narrative to others in the Circle of Adults session who likely have faced or will face a similar challenge to their disciplinary authority and who might want to respond in an equally creative way.

BEFORE RUNNING THE CIRCLE OF ADULTS SESSION

Before Setting up a Circle of Adults, prerequisites that should be in place are:

- Agreement from senior managers in a school that this work will take place and be supported.

- A group of staff commit to attend a number of sessions. An initial session may be needed to demonstrate the nature and power of this process. Following this a series of sessions should be agreed. Between four and eight sessions on a regular basis across one school term would be rich for developmental or professional development purposes. Building the process into ongoing pastoral processes of staff and pupil support and guidance, a much bigger goal, would be even more likely to facilitate major change across a school system.

- A place to meet which is safe from interruption, offering some privacy, a true 'place to be', or 'place to talk'. Key factors include some degree of quiet, comfortable seating, low lighting, a clear wall space that a large piece of graphic paper can be taped to.

- Time to meet. Possibly the toughest requirement in today's overheated school weeks. At least 90 minutes is required to do such a meeting real justice.

- Two facilitators available to lead the sessions. Initially these may well be recruited from outside agencies visiting schools, such as psychologists and behaviour support teachers. Longer term, the aim should be to develop the skills in-house to run such sessions. Year managers or other senior pastoral teachers could take on such a facilitation role, following the described processes, with training, support and preparation. Support and supervision for such leaders would also be extremely useful and desirable if not essential.

- A graphic as well as process facilitator.

YOUR NOTES

We have found it helpful in the early stages of learning to facilitate a Circle of Adults session to have a 'crib sheet' to hand. This page is a photocopiable sheet for just this purpose. It lists the 10 key steps of the process with spaces for you to add your own reminders and prompts. This is particularly valuable for the process facilitator. The graphic facilitator also needs to keep one eye on process and ensure that nothing is missed and that all the steps are followed. It is easy to get lost in the content during a circle of adults session, even for experienced facilitators, and it helps if both facilitators are taking responsibility for managing process.

1. Agree GROUND RULES for the session to come.

2. PRESENT PROBLEM.

3. EXPLORE RELATIONSHIPS.

4. Consider ORGANISATIONAL FACTORS that help or hinder the problem situation.

5. Listen to what the CHILD'S VOICE has to say.

6. Listen to a SYNTHESIS of all that have been recorded so far.

7. Generate HYPOTHESES that help make sense of what is happening.

8. Generate STRATEGIES linked to the hypotheses.

9. Agree some FIRST STEPS the problem presenter can take in the very near future and appoint a coach to check these have been done by an agreed time.

10. The session closes with a summary comment from each participant - a 'ROUND OF WORDS'.

REFERENCES and Recommended Reading

Andersen, T. (Ed.) (1991) *The Reflecting Team.* New York: Norton

Bettelhiem, B. and Rosenfeld, A. (1993) *The Art of the Obvious - Developing Insight for Psychotherapy and Everyday Life.* London: Thames and Hudson

Evans, S. (2005) *The Development of a Group Consultation Approach to Service Delivery 'Educational Psychology in Practice'*, Vol. 21, No. 2, pp. 131-146

Farouk, S. (2004) *Group Work in Schools: A process consultation approach. Educational Psychology in Practice*, Vol. 20, No.3 September 2004

Gill, D. & Monsen, J. (1995) The staff sharing scheme: a school based management system for working with challenging child behaviour. *Educational and Child Psychology*, 12(2), 71-80

Gill, D. &Monsen, J (1996) A school based management system for working with challenging child behaviour. In E.Blyth & J Milner (Eds) *Exclusion from School: inter-professional issues for policy and practice.* London: Routledge.

Hanko, G. (2002) Making psychodynamic insights accessible to teachers as an integral part of their professional task. *Psychodynamic Practice* 8.3 August.

Hoffman, L. (2002) *Family Therapy - An Intimate History*. New York: Norton

Holman, P. and Devane, T. (1999) *The Change Handbook*. San Francisco, Berrett-Koehler Publishers.

Kaner, S. et al (1996) *Facilitator's Guide to Participatory Decision-Making*. Canada, New Society Publishers.

Lovett, H. (1996) *Learning to Listen - Positive Approaches and People with Difficult Behaviour.* Baltimore: Paul Brookes Publishing.

Moore, J. (2005) Recognising and Questioning the Epistemological Basis of Educational Psychology Practice. *Educational Psychology in Practice*, Vol. 21, No. 2. Pp.103- 116.

Newton, C. (1995) Circles of Adults. *Educational Psychology in Practice*, Vol. 11 (2), pp 8-14

Nias, J., Southworth G and Yeoman, R (1989) *Staff Relationships in the Primary School: a study of organisational culture.* London: Cassell.

O'Brien, J. (1995) 'Inclusion as a Force for School Renewal' in Stainback, W. and Stainback, S. (eds.) *Inclusion a Guide for Educators.* Baltimore: Paul Brookes Publishing

O'Brien, J. (2002) 'An Inclusive School' Plenary address at the Inclusion Now Summer School July 2002 Nottingham.

O'Brien, J. and O'Brien, C. (2002) *Implementing Person Centred Planning*. Toronto: Inclusion Press.
Available from www.inclusive-solutions.com

Owen, H. (1997) *Open Space Technology - A User's Guide*. Second Edition San Francisco: Berrett-Koehler Publishers

Pearpoint, J. (2002) *Hints for Graphic Facilitators*. Toronto: Inclusion Press
Available from www.inclusive-solutions.com

Pearpoint, J., O'Brien, J. and Forest, M. (2001) *Path - A Workbook for Planning Positive Possible Futures* - 2nd edition. Toronto: Inclusion Press
Available from www.inclusive-solutions.com

Remen, Rachel Naomi. (1996) *Kitchen Table Wisdom - Stories That Heal* . London: Pan Books

Sibbet, D. (2002) *Best Practices for Facilitation.* San Francisco: The Grove Consultants International, www.grove.com

Sinason, V. (1992) *Mental Handicap and the Human Condition.*
London: Free Association Books

Sonneman, M. (1997) *Beyond Words - A Guide to Drawing Out Ideas.* Berkeley, California: Ten Speed Press

Spohrer, K. and Cooke, C. (2005) A Problem Shared. *Including Special Children. Issue 166 Pp 27-29.*

Stockley, S. (2003) *Circles of Adults: An exploration of an experiential process to develop teachers' emotional and professional competency.* Dissertation submitted to the University of Nottingham in partial fulfilment of the requirements for Master of Arts in Human Relations, University of Nottingham.

CD ROMs

PowerPoint presentations

1. **Colin and Derek's original 'Circles of Friends' Slideshow** is now also available.

This slideshow can be used to support training on inclusion and Circles of Friends.
This CD also has a short video welcome and a short description of how to set up circles in schools.

Price £30 (Post and Packaging £2.50)

2. **Boys Emotional Needs**

This original Slideshow is now also available.
This slideshow can be used to support training on inclusion and the meeting of emotional needs.
This CD also has a short video welcome.

Price £30 (Post and Packaging £2.50)

VIDEOS

1. **'Circle of Adults'**.

This package comes with a booklet detailing the process. Process for detailed in depth problem solving around complex individuals. The video shows the key steps being used live with a diverse group of educators in Nottingham.

Price £30 (Post and Packaging £2.50)

2. **'Circles of Friends'**

Video is now available showing two circles in action. This resource brings to life Circles in a fresh and appealing way. Listen to young people reflecting on their circle experiences.

Price £30 (Post and Packaging £2.50)

TRAINING OPPORTUNITIES FOR YOUR CONSIDERATION

We can adapt any of this training to suit the needs of your team or organization.

KEYS to INCLUSION

This is our lead workshop/training day and is both a values primer and a practical guide to successful strategies for developing inclusive practice in educational settings for children and young people of all ages. Best delivered over the course of a full day, 'Keys to Inclusion' introduces participants to 6 guiding Ideas that underpin inclusive practice.

- The importance of WELCOME
- Inclusion is about Adults' learning
- Taking the Long View
- Giftedness as a new paradigm for understanding disability and difference
- The Intentional Building of Relationships – 'Circle of Friends' work as an example of this
- Not doing it alone – The Importance of Teams in developing inclusive practice

Outcomes:

1. increased confidence regarding developing inclusive practice in mainstream schools
2. access to a wider range of practical strategies to impact on behaviour problems
3. deeper understanding of core values surrounding inclusion of disabled children
4. opportunity to reflect on professional attitudes and behaviour towards parents and pupils
5. learn new skills and processes to make inclusion successful

INCLUDING CHILDREN WITH AUTISM IN MAINSTREAM SETTINGS

In this practical workshop session we will explore ways of including pupils who have been labelled as being on the autism spectrum. The session will be values based and practical and will aim to allow the sharing of experiences and good practice as well promoting innovative approaches to inclusion through the design of best practice. Parental perspectives and experiences will also be explored.

Key themes include:

- Learning Styles and Curriculum Modifications
- Strategies for Facilitating Communication
- Supports and Accommodations for Sensory Sensitivities
- Developing Friendships and Peer Support
- School and Family Partnerships
- 'Learning to Listen' – Positive Behavioural Supports
- Developing School wide Supports for Teachers and Students

Outcomes:

- increased confidence regarding autistic pupils and their inclusion in mainstream schools
- access to a wider range of practical strategies to impact on communication and behaviour issues
- deeper understanding of core values surrounding inclusion
- learn new skills and processes to make inclusion of autistic pupils successful

INCLUSIVE LEARNING AND TEACHING STYLES

What makes an inclusive classroom?

This workshop/training day and is a practical guide to successful strategies for developing inclusive learning preferences and teaching styles in educational settings for children and young people of all ages. In this very interactive workshop we will explore what it takes to fully engage, educate and motivate young people with a wide range of needs and differences.

- The importance of WELCOME and Setting the tone for learning
- Visual Learning styles
- Auditory and musical Learning
- The 3 Kinaesthetic styles and how to access them
- Multiple intelligences
- Giftedness as a new paradigm for teaching and learning
- Diversifying the curriculum
- Creating a vision of the accessible curriculum and community classroom

Outcomes:

1. increased confidence regarding developing inclusive practice in mainstream schools
2. access to a wider range of practical strategies to impact on teaching and learning
3. deeper understanding of link between teaching and learning and whole school improvement
4. opportunity to reflect on professional practice
5. learn new skills and processes to make inclusion successful

BUILDING CREATIVE STAFF TEAMS

Want ideas as to how to make your team work together more effectively?
Need to know how to make your team feel more inclusive to its members?

In this practical and engaging workshop there is input on team building, problem solving as a team, improving communication and handling conflict. How to make teams really inclusive is fully explored and processes for maximising this examined. Effective leadership and management, which can transform teamwork through collaboration and consensus-building processes is well covered. We will explore the following:

1. Setting the tone
2. Visioning
3. Locating gifts in one another
4. Building consensus
5. Problem solving
6. Building the team community
7. Self care and survival
8. Closure

COLLABORATIVE WORKING BETWEEN PARENTS/CARERS AND SENCOs IN THE EARLY YEARS

In this practical and engaging workshop there is input on building an effective team around a child, problem solving as a team, improving communication and handling conflict. How to make teams really inclusive is fully explored and processes for maximising this examined. Effective co-leadership and management, which can transform teamwork through collaboration and consensus-building processes is covered. We will explore the following:

1. Setting the tone
2. Visioning
3. Locating gifts in one another
4. Building consensus
5. Problem solving
6. Building the team
7. Self care and survival

INCLUDING ALL PUPILS IN SECONDARY SCHOOLS

This challenging workshop will provide participants with opportunities to share experiences and learn about the successful inclusion of pupils with severe and complex disabilities as well as emotional and behavioural needs in mainstream secondary schools. Cutting edge work being carried out in the US as well as the UK will be drawn upon to allow innovative and engaging content.

The session will be of particular value to heads, deputies, Heads of Learning Support and other involved middle managers plus those agencies that work with schools (e.g. social services working with Children in Need and Children and Young People in Public Care; Child and Adolescent Mental Health services; community paediatricians etc).

LEADERSHIP FOR INCLUSION

In this session we will explore the challenges faced by leaderships of schools when tackling inclusion issues. We develop the concept of the leader as being central to the web of an organisation, the web of inclusion. Information flows freely to and from the leaders and interconnections are a premium. We will also cover a range of areas including:

- Vision and values
- Trust
- Creating inclusive staff teams and communities of acceptance
- Admissions and welcome
- Creative problem solving
- Organisational models
- Curriculum access and curriculum design for inclusion
- Work with parents
- Consensus building

Areas covered in this session will build on the work described in 'TEAMS FOR INCLUSION – What should they be doing and What should they not be doing?' Published in 'Special Children', October 2002

FRESH APPROACHES TO MANAGING CHALLENGING BEHAVIOUR

If your usual approaches to managing behaviour aren't working with particular individuals then...

Take a tour through this range of cutting edge strategies for bringing about positive behaviour change, and for meeting challenging emotional needs:

- Circles of adults: a process that 'listens deeper' to generate reflective problem solving creating lasting behaviour change and effective behaviour intervention plans. A particularly valuable process for those looking to enhance their leadership and facilitation skills
- Circles of friends: peer support and inclusion. Pupils work to problem solve with and actively support the inclusion and behaviour change of one of their peers
- Peer support, counselling and mediation: reduce bullying and address emotional needs as older pupils offer active listening support and interventions
- Solution circles: a 30 minute group problem solving process to get Teams 'unstuck' and to generate positive first action steps
- Giving boys what they need: focus on particular strategies for meeting the emotional needs of boys
- Restorative justice and restitution: principles and practice of this approach to resolving and restoring relationships without reliance on punishment
- Community networks of support: creating ownership of the solutions in local mainstream schools made more therapeutic

Outcomes:

1. Reinforce good practice
2. re-energise, stimulate and challenge thinking about inclusion and behaviour
3. increased understanding about behaviour
4. increased confidence in managing challenging pupils in mainstream schools
5. access to a wider range of practical strategies to impact on behaviour problems
6. deeper understanding of core values surrounding inclusion of challenging pupils
7. opportunity to reflect on professional attitudes and behaviour towards families and pupils
8. learn new skills and processes to make inclusion successful

CIRCLES OF FRIENDS – Introductory/intermediate/advanced

An inclusive approach to meeting emotional and behavioural needs

What do you do with the child who is isolated by their aggression and anger, through being different, disabled or new to the school or community?

Circle of Friends is an approach to enhancing the inclusion, in a mainstream setting, of any young person who is experiencing difficulties in school because of a disability, personal crisis or because of their challenging behaviour towards others. The 'circle of friends' approach works by mobilising the young person's peers to provide support and engage in problem solving with the person in difficulty.

'Circle of friends' is not the same as 'circle time' but many of the skills and techniques used by teachers in 'circle time' can be used to support the 'circle of friends' process. Over the past 10 years Colin Newton and Derek Wilson have been encouraging the use of 'circle of friends' in a wide variety of primary and secondary schools, often with very successful outcomes, some of which are described in their book 'Circles of Friends', (Folens, 1999).

This is an excellent opportunity to learn from Colin Newton and Derek Wilson the educational psychologists who brought this DfES endorsed approach to the UK

Learn how to build teams around challenging pupils by drawing on a resource which is always there.... other children. Enjoy participating in a multi media workshop that will challenge, entertain and reach for your emotions. Circles of support are for us all, for life....and they work!

Outcomes:

1. to be able to understand the values and wider context of inclusion
2. to be able to set up and run a 'circle of friends' to reduce likelihood of a pupil being excluded or segregated
3. to understand and be able to maximise the power of the peer group in supporting relationships, achievement and behaviour change

CIRCLES OF ADULTS

Teams reflecting and problem solving about emotional and behavioural needs at a deeper level

Cannot understand why a child is behaving as they do?

Struggling with a child for whom praise is ineffective?

Feeling isolated in your responses to a child's needs?

Worried about where your instinctive reactions are leading you?

Dealing with strong personal feelings, which are getting in the way of your reactions to a pupil?

Cannot seem to get any consensus view of a young person's behaviour/needs amongst all the professionals involved – everyone pulling in different directions?

Learn a deeper approach to problem solving which will provide you with a new and richer approach to developing inclusive strategies for dealing with the most difficult to reach children and young people. Reflect on your own emotional responses to individuals you work with, explore relationships and generate richer hypotheses about what is really going on.

Outcomes:

1. deeper understanding of what is actually happening underneath the behaviour and to maintain problems
2. increased confidence in managing challenging pupils in mainstream schools
3. process for locating richer and wider range of practical strategies to impact on behaviour problems
4. deeper understanding of inclusion of challenging pupils
5. opportunity to reflect on professional practice
6. mutual support established with other 'front line' practitioners

PERSON CENTRED PLANNING – using PATH and MAPs

Making inclusive action plans using full participation and graphic facilitation

Need to find new ways to bring Pathway Planning alive?

Bored with annual reviews, transition plans and review meetings?

Want to find a way of making meetings and planning feel more real and engaging?

Need an approach, which engages a young person respectfully together with his or her family and friends?

Want the ultimate visual record of the process of a meeting, which will help everyone, keep track?

Want to problem solve and plan for the future of a small or large group, service or organisation up to the size of an LEA?

Learn how to carry out respectful person centred planning involving a diverse group of people and a big piece of paper!

Jack Pearpoint, Marsha Forest and John O'Brien developed these innovative approaches in North America and they are beginning to be used successfully in parts of the UK. The planning can focus on an individual, group or organisation and provides a powerful problem solving opportunity, which is flexible and robust enough for many occasions. Tell the story, find the dream, touch the nightmare, and explore who you are, what are the gifts and strengths of the person or group, what are the needs of those present and what is the action plan for the future?

There is a useful phrase in 'Implementing Person Centred Planning – Voices of Experience' John O'Brien and Connie Lyle O'Brien (Eds) Inclusion Press 2002 that is a good description of what we are trying to create when we bring groups together over a period of time to learn Person Centred Planning or Circles of Adults or other inclusive tools, what we are building is a 'community of practice'. Communities of practice are: groups of people who share a concern, a set of problems, or a passion about a topic, and who deepen their knowledge and expertise in this area interacting on an ongoing basis (Wenger and Snyder 2000, Communities of Practice – Harvard Business Review)

It might also be useful to note that 'Valuing People' (Department of Health, 2002 pp 13-14), defines the 5 key features of PCP as:

- The person is at the centre
- Family members and friends are full partners
- Planning reflects the person's capacities, what is important to the person and specifies the support they require to make a full contribution to their community
- Planning builds a shared commitment to action that will uphold the person's rights
- Planning leads to continual listening, learning and action and helps the person get what they want out of life.

The challenge is to develop/learn to use tools that make these outcomes more likely. The most common planning tools in use in the UK include Essential Lifestyle Planning, PATH, MAPS and Personal Futures Planning.

Inclusive Solutions offer an introductory day to person centred planning or a 10 session course which is practical as well as values based. Participants will receive direct individualised coaching and training.

Outcomes

1. Participants understand Person centred planning and its values and applications
2. Participants have skills and confidence to facilitate PATH/MAP processes
3. Participants learn graphic as well as process facilitation skills.
4. Strengthens practitioners inclusive practice
5. Provides additional tools for those involved in inclusive work in schools and the community
6. Further developed problem solving and planning skills for use with individuals, groups and schools.

MEETING THE EMOTIONAL NEEDS OF BOYS

Working together to understand and better meet boy's emotional and behavioural needs

This workshop gives an opportunity to focus on the emotional needs of boys and how to meet these. The workshop will explore:

- Cultural and historical expectations of boys in our society
- Shared experiences of teaching and parenting boys
- Fathers and sons
- Mothers and sons
- Drinking and drugs, filling the emotional void
- Depression and suicide
- Relationships with girls
- Anger and violence
- What boys really need

MEETING THE NEEDS OF CHILDREN IN PUBLIC CARE – introductory/intermediate/advanced

An overview of the needs of young people in public care and provides examples of how these needs can be met. These workshops can explore:

- Story so far – educational underachievement and social exclusion
- Causes of underachievement and social exclusion
- Current initiatives
- Case studies
- Multi-agency working
- Corporate Parenting
- Designated Teachers
- Personal Education Plans
- Resilience – factors promoting success
- Peer support/mentoring
- Young people's views
- Circles of adults
- MAPS and PATH
- Circles of friends

These workshops will be of interest to teachers, designated teachers, social workers, residential social workers, foster carers, education support services, Local Authority Managers and other organisations working with young people in public care (e.g. Child and Adolescent Mental Health Services, Youth Workers etc.)

PEER COUNSELLING AS AN ANTI-BULLYING STRATEGY

Key Themes covered within the training include:

- Issues of Confidentiality
- Welcoming your client
- Using active listening skills
- Using Open and Closed Questions to enable your client to tell you his or her story
- How to reflect back feelings and how to check you have understood what the client has told you
- Exploring options for resolving the bullying issue with your client

LIVE VISIONING AND PROBLEM SOLVING

PATH or MAP processes carried out with groups, families and large organisations of up to 200 people. Dynamic visioning work with graphic facilitation and active leadership. Half day or full day sessions available to focus on small or large issues with all the right people present. We have tools to help you get unstuck and to develop consensus around complex areas.

Let us join you to explore your vision and help remove the 'roadblocks' to your vision.

'TRAINING THE TRAINERS'

Training and Support Package

- Building Capacity for Inclusion
- Planning for Inclusion
- Staff Development and Training

This training package is aimed at developing the skills and knowledge of a locally based core group of trainers who would then in turn be able to offer training across your area.

This work would allow trainers to offer workshop/training days, both values primers and practical guides to successful strategies for developing inclusive practice in educational settings for children and young people of all ages. These will form the building blocks/initial stages of efforts to provide training and continuous professional development for teachers and other school staff to support inclusion

Our 'Training the trainers' inputs will introduce participants to a range of guiding ideas, each with their associated practical strategies that underpin inclusive practice.

The key strands of these inputs with an indication of content are as follows:

- The importance of Welcome and Listening in the Inclusive Classroom this strand will explore how inclusive schools need to set the tone for learning by establishing a sense of safety and belonging. We will introduce the 4 essential similarities between all learners:

1. Everyone needs to work things out for themselves
2. Experiences that multi-sensory, dramatic, unusual or emotionally strong are remembered for longer and in more detail than, ordinary, routine experiences
3. Everyone needs to feel emotionally secure and psychologically safe
4. Learners are more motivated, engaged and open when they have some control over their learning

continued opposite

- We will look at a range of ways these principles can be put into practice and will also examine teacher practices that support the building of classroom community.
- Capacity Building as a new paradigm for understanding disability and difference and an exploration of how school record keeping and paperwork systems can reflect person centred recording and planning.
- Teaching and Learning in the Inclusive Classroom: a range of models that develop teachers' understanding of learning styles and preferences will be explored – principally those based on Sensory preferences: visual, auditory, kinaesthetic, those based on cognitive predilections (Gregorc's 'Mindstyles' analysis) and those based on intelligence profiles (Howard Gardner's Multiple Intelligence Theory) on inclusive teaching and accommodations, uses of peer support. This strand will also look in depth at inclusive lesson planning using the following ' fundamental questions' as a guide:

1. What is the essential knowledge to be gained?
2. How do my students learn best?
3. What modifications to a lesson would permit more students to learn effectively in my classroom?
4. How will my students show what they have learned?

This simple rubric is highly effective in enabling teachers to think constructively about how to meet the needs of all learners including those with significant impairments.

- The Intentional Building of Relationships within the Inclusive Classroom – 'Restorative Interventions' and 'Circle of Friends' work as an example of this. Participants will have confidence in the setting up and running a variety of peer support interventions and in training others to do so as a result of these inputs
- Not Doing It Alone – The Importance of Teams in developing inclusive practice. This strand will explore the use of a range of process tools (Solution Circles, Circle of Adults, MAPS) that enable effective multi-agency Teamwork. Membership and role within the Inclusive team will be explored with a particular emphasis on the role of auxiliaries.
- Taking the Long View: this strand will address the need for inclusive planning to take a holistic approach to the long term needs of the child and his or her family. It will look at a range of Person-Centred planning tools e.g. PATH, Essential Lifestyle Planning, Personal Futures Planning and consider how these can inform the development of inclusive practice in schools especially at key transition points.

Outcomes:

1. Training providers create a training package/range of training packages to support your Inclusion Strategy
2. Increased confidence regarding developing inclusive practice in mainstream schools
3. Access to a wider range of practical strategies to impact on behaviour problems
4. Deeper understanding of core values surrounding the inclusion of disabled children and those with SEN
5. Opportunity to reflect on professional attitudes and behaviour towards parents and pupils and an enhanced understanding of how change in school practice can be initiated and supported
6. Learn and reflect on a range new skills and processes to make inclusion successful
7. Trainers will have knowledge of and be able to access a range of written and other resources: Books, Websites, Video materials, Planning Tools for further use in their training
8. Trainers will be supported in the development and use of a range of approaches to training delivery e.g. effective use of PowerPoint presentations, use of video in training, use of Graphic Facilitation in building consensus and shared vision in staff groups, ensuring training inputs are participative and thus model inclusive practice.

continued overleaf

Process:

1. Recruit Trainers(Inclusive Solutions involvement is optional)
2. 5 day intensive training and package production with target team of Training providers
3. Trainers will require time to prepare and trial materials emerging from this work (Approx 2 days)
4. Day with Inclusive Solutions to fine tune emerging work materials/package
5. Implementation of training across your area
6. Day of problem solving, evaluation and reflection with Inclusive Solutions

Other training titles include:

Building inclusive LEA teams

Solution circles

Graphic Facilitation

Peer Mentoring

Phone us at: 0115 9556045, 0115 9408550 or 0115 9605071
Email us at: inclusive.solutions@ntlworld.com
Web site: www.inclusive-solutions.com
Write to us at 49 Northcliffe Avenue, Nottingham, NG3 6DA

Colin Newton and Derek Wilson
Co-Founders
Inclusive Solutions